THE BUSINESS ADMINIS
AND DIARY NVQ

LEVELS I AND II

THE BUSINESS ADMINISTRATION HANDBOOK AND DIARY NVQ

LEVELS I AND II

Sue Kennedy

McGRAW-HILL Book Company

London · New York · St Louis · San Francisco · Auckland
· Bogatà · Caracas · Hamburg · Lisbon · Madrid· Mexico
· Milan · Montreal · New Delhi · Panama · Paris · San Juan
· São Paulo · Singapore · Sydney · Tokyo · Toronto

Published by

McGRAW-HILL BOOK COMPANY EUROPE

SHOPPENHANGERS ROAD, MAIDENHEAD, BERKSHIRE, SL6 2QL, ENGLAND
Telephone 0628 23432
Fax 0628 770224

British Library Cataloguing in Publication Data

Kennedy, Sue
  The business administration handbook and diary
  NVQ levels I and II.
  I. Title
  658.10941

  ISBN 0–07–707299–5

1234CUP9432

Typeset by TecSet Ltd, Wallington, Surrey
and printed and bound in Great Britain at the University Press, Cambridge

CONTENTS

DIARY PAGES

REFERENCE GUIDES

INDEX

ACKNOWLEDGEMENTS

The author would like to thank the following for their kind permission to reproduce materials with this text:
British Telecom Business Communications
The Post Office
The TSB Bank
The Controller of Her Majesty's Stationery Office
Brimley & Co Ltd.

INTRODUCTION

This book has been specifically written for candidates undertaking a National Vocational Qualification in Business Administration at Level 1 or 2, but is also suitable for anyone wishing to train for a career in an office. It is hoped that the information contained in the handbook will provide the underpinning knowledge so necessary before tasks can be performed. Though the handbook covers all areas of the qualification, it is expected that those candidates who choose the financial option may require further instruction on the principles of bookkeeping.

It has also been written to provide a useful office handbook to be kept in the workplace.

To be awarded an NVQ it is necessary to show that you can carry out tasks, over a period of time. It is therefore very important to keep a record of all tasks performed correctly that are relevant to the qualification, as once you can provide evidence that you are competent at carrying out a task you can actually claim competence. When your tutor or supervisor feels that you have sufficient evidence to claim competence then you have to complete the competence transcript provided by the examination board. The Diary element of this book has been designed to help you record this evidence in as simple a manner as possible. Complete it in your own words every day, or as frequently as possible, just as you would keep your own diary. By completing all the information requested you are already showing competence in using information sources and completing records.

BUSINESS ADMINISTRATION: AN OVERVIEW

To say that you work in an office, or you would like to work in an office, are very vague statements, because offices vary tremendously. For example, offices may be very small or very large; they may be modern and up to date or quite the opposite; and the work of an office will vary depending upon the type of organization you are working for.

There are many different types of organization you could work for: a manufacturing company, a retailing company, a bank or financial institution, a construction company, a solicitor, a local government or a hospital, to name but a few. Although this large variety of organizations exists, it is true to say that whichever one you choose there will be a considerable amount of administrative work to be done.

► ADMINISTRATIVE STRUCTURE AND FUNCTIONS

To be successful in an office you must first understand:

1 What we mean by **administration**.

2 How organizations are **structured** so that they run efficiently.

Let us start by looking at these two points.

Administration

This is a term we use to cover the work that needs to be done so that an organization runs efficiently. This involves such tasks as:

- Communicating with people.
- Storing and gathering information.
- Keeping financial records.
- Reproducing documents.
- Ordering and supplying goods and services.

Many people would define administration as 'paper work' and indeed written records do need to be kept so that certain people within and outside the organization know exactly what is happening. This paper work involves many skills, not only numeracy, communication and keyboarding, but also skills in dealing with people and creating good relationships with fellow colleagues and customers/clients. This will make your job much more enjoyable. Modern offices now have electronic equipment to help with administration and you will need to learn how to operate this equipment safely and efficiently.

As an example, consider some of the administrative functions involved with manufacturing a motor car.

1 The company must research and plan how many cars they need to produce.

2 The car must be designed.

3 Staff need to be appointed to make the product and run the company.

4 Equipment and parts have to be ordered and paid for.

5 The finished product has to be marketed and sold.

6 Wages will need to be paid.

7 Records must be kept of all the above plans, decisions and functions.

If the administration is not carried out correctly, then the company is likely to run in to serious financial difficulties.

Structure of an organization

Any organization needs to have a structure. Large companies, small companies, Government Institutions, voluntary organizations, such as The St John's Ambulance Brigade, national and local clubs and societies, all need a structure. Someone has to be in charge and the work has to be divided so that members of the organization know exactly what they are expected to do and to whom they are responsible.

All organizations are different. You will find that Government Institutions have a different structure to companies and no two companies will have exactly the same structure. It may be helpful to look at a selection of examples: a college, a small family-run business and a large manufacturing company, and to compare the differences in personnel and departments. These examples (Figures 1.1, 1.2 and 1.3) show the senior people at the top of the chart to demonstrate the line of responsibility. Most organization charts will be shown in this way.

Note:
When you go to work for an organization it is worth while trying to find out the structure of the organization and who is your supervisor or 'boss': this could save a great deal of embarrassment.

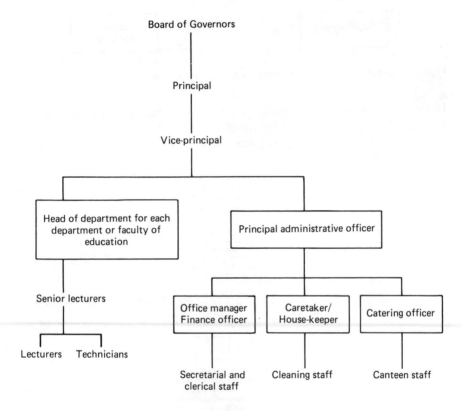

Figure 1.1 *Organizational chart of a typical college of further education*

Each department may have secretarial/clerical support. All colleges have a general office where general administrative duties will be performed, ie reception, switchboard, mail handling, in addition to tasks that will enable the college to run smoothly, eg examination entries, purchasing of stationery and equipment, appointment of staff.

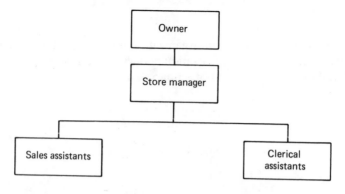

Figure 1.2 *Organizational chart of a small family run grocery business*

In the situation shown in Figure 1.2 you may be the only clerical assistant, responsible for all administrative functions, related to buying, selling, financial record keeping, and personnel, under the supervision of the store manager and/or owner.

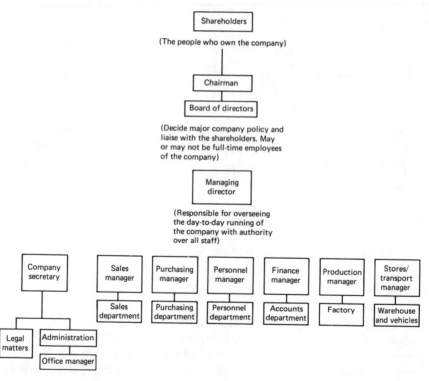

Figure 1.3 *Organizational chart of a large manufacturing company*

Table 1.1   Functions of each department

Administration Dept responsible for:	Purchasing Dept responsible for:	Sales Dept responsible for:	Accounts Dept responsible for:	Personnel Dept responsible for:
Typing/secretarial	Finding suppliers of goods required	Advertising products/ services	Ensuring all financial transactions are recorded and accurate records are kept	Advertising vacancies for jobs
Data processing	Sending letters of enquiry and requesting price lists/catalogues to ensure the best terms	Liaising with customers/ clients: giving information on products	Maintaining the cash flow of the company, ie ensuring there is sufficient money coming in to meet all outgoings	Appointing staff
Switchboard		Preparing quotations		Keeping staff records
Reception				Training employees
Mail room	Ordering all goods, eg raw materials, office equipment, stationery and completing the necessary paperwork	Selling goods and preparing paper work	Ensuring all bills sent to the company are paid and all money owed to the company is collected promptly	Negotiating with trade unions
Filing		Dealing with exports (selling goods abroad)		Dealing with resignations and dismissals
Reprographics		Providing a back-up service for customers	Preparing financial budgets and forecasts	Promoting employees
Legal matters	Dealing with imports (buying goods in from abroad)		Preparing the payroll and paying wages and salaries	Dealing with staff problems, ie sickness, grievances
	Keeping records of all money spent		Supervising petty cash	Ensuring good working conditions Health and Safety
	Stock control: to ensure that too many goods are not purchased, but there is always a sufficient quantity in hand		Credit control, ie ensuring customers do not owe too much money	Organizing social events in the interest of staff welfare

In the situation shown in Figure 1.3 you would be working in one of the departments undertaking a specific role, ie reprographics clerk, invoicing clerk, receptionist.

When you work for a large company you need to know what each department does; it is not wise to be isolated in your own job. If you work for example as a receptionist, switchboard operator, mail room assistant or reprographics clerk then it is essential that you are familiar with the work of each department, so that you know who to route enquiries and correspondence to.

Table 1.1 is a guide to the functions each department will perform.

> **REMEMBER!** A company may have additional departments carrying out some of the above duties, ie training may be a separate department and the above is only a guide.

Having looked at the main administrative functions carried out by each department, the following sections of this handbook will give you help and information on carrying out these functions. However, you will soon realize that the work of departments is interrelated and it is difficult to perform one administrative task without involving others. This is why it is important to create and maintain good working relationships, as you may need to rely on the assistance of fellow employees and good teamwork.

► HEALTH AND SAFETY IN THE OFFICE

Accidents can happen **anywhere** and the office is no exception. We think of the office as being a healthy and safe environment to work in, and it can be if certain steps are taken by the employer and employee to make it so.

In 1963 the Office, Shops and Railway Premises Act was introduced which ensured that the owner of the premises met standards laid down by the Government with regard to cleanliness, temperature (the room temperature should not be less than 16° C after the first hour), ventilation, lighting, sanitary conveniences, washing facilities, overcrowding (each employee is entitled to 3.7 m² of floor space) and other facilities required for the general welfare of staff.

In 1974 the Health and Safety at Work Act was introduced that strengthened the previous act by placing responsibilities for health and safety on the **employee** as well as the employer (see Figure 1.4). For this reason all employees must be made aware of the act. This act is enforced by health and

Figure 1.4 *Office mishaps*

safety inspectors. In 1981 new regulations were introduced regarding first-aid at work and in 1988 COSHH was introduced that relates to the Control of Substances Hazardous to Health.

If there are five or more employees, the employer must draw up a health and safety policy statement informing the employee of the organization's arrangements for protecting your health.

NOTICE

Your health, safety and welfare at work are protected by law. Your employer has a duty to protect you and to keep you informed about health and safety. You have a responsibility to look after yourself and others. If there is a problem, discuss it with your employer or your safety representative if there is one.

Fire

Employers have duties to take precautions against fire, provide adequate means of escape and means for fighting fire. They should ensure all employees know what to do in the case of fire.

How?

1 By providing instruction and training on the organization's emergency procedure, building layout and fire fighting equipment.

2 By ensuring that notices of the evacuation procedure are posted around the building.

3 By ensuring that escape routes are clearly labelled.

4 By checking that the fire alarm system is adequate. Testing the alarm at intervals and making sure that all employees can hear it are important.

5 By making sure that personnel know their responsibilities: who is responsible for checking that the building is empty, eg toilets, and who is responsible for phoning the emergency services.

6 By installing the correct fire fighting equipment and instructing staff on how to use it. The local fire service will give assistance and advice here on items such as automatic water sprinkler systems, fire extinguishers for use on electrical equipment, water hoses, sand buckets, fire blankets.

As an employee **you** must ensure that you know the organization's fire and evacuation procedure and do your utmost to prevent fire. What can **you** do?

1 Keep fire doors closed.

2 Keep gangways and passages clear.

3 Ensure that waste paper bins are emptied regularly.

4 Observe **no smoking** areas.

5 Extinguish cigarettes properly using an ashtray.

6 Store any inflammable materials in a locked cupboard or storeroom, ensuring that they are clearly labelled.

7 Take care with electric fires: make sure they are not close to anything that may catch fire.

8 Do not overload plug sockets with electrical appliances. Report any problems with the equipment promptly. Unless instructed otherwise, switch off and unplug electrical equipment at night.

Accidents

Many accidents occurring in the office may be minor, requiring no more than a small plaster, but some may require urgent medical attention. Remember that prevention is better than cure. Again it is the responsibility of both your employer and **you** to do as much as possible to prevent accidents. Table 1.2 is a guide to what you can both do.

Accidents and medical emergencies can occur however safety conscious an organization is and therefore the Health and Safety (First-Aid) Regulations 1981 and the Code of Practice revised in July 1990 requires employers to provide adequate first-aid facilities. First-aid boxes that are accessible to all staff must be provided and all staff must be informed where the box is and who is responsible for it. If a first-aid box is not available in each room then notices must be posted stating where it is. The first-aid box must conform to the 1981 Health and Safety (First-Aid) Regulations. Contents should include plasters, triangular bandage, eye pads, safety pins, assorted dressings. In offices employers need to provide one first-aider during normal working hours for every 50 employees: this means that if there are only two employees one should be responsible for the first-aid box and be trained to 'react in a crisis situation', ie know how to dial 999 and preferably have a basic knowledge of first-aid. However these are only guidelines and the employer must use common sense with regard to the number of trained first-aid staff

Table 1.2   Accident prevention

Employer's responsibilities	Employee's responsibilities
Ensure that all electrical equipment is correctly installed. Plug fitted correctly and earthed. Ample plug sockets to prevent overloading and trailing wires.	Avoid trailing wires. Ensure that the equipment is located in a safe position. Switch off when not in use. Report faults promptly. If the equipment is out of order, leave a notice on the machine to this effect. Do not repair electrical equipment yourself.
Ensure furniture and fittings are well maintained and safe, eg floor coverings are not worn.	Do not leave drawers open. Do not overload the top drawer of a filing cabinet, so it becomes 'top heavy'. Do not stand on furniture, particularly swivel chairs, to reach heights. Report any problems to your supervisor or health and safety representative.
Provide adequate lighting and heating as laid down in the Office, Shops and Railway Premises Act.	Ensure you work in good light. Avoid using electric fires for additional heating. Seek permission if you do. Never use an unguarded electric fire. Ensure adequate ventilation: lack of ventilation can lead to tiredness and accidents.
Provide suitable instruction and training on lifting heavy objects, looking after your own and other people's safety.	Use any protective clothing/items that have been provided for your safety, ie rubber gloves, step stools, staple extractors. Follow safety instructions you have been given. Do not block corridors or walkways, even temporarily and keep doorways clear. Use your common sense, ie if you spill liquid on the floor, then mop it up immediately.

employed. Offices can be prosecuted for not providing adequate first-aid cover and though the Health and Safety Executive enforce the regulations in Local Government Offices, it is the Environmental Health Department that enforces the Act for offices and shops.

Accident book

Alongside every first-aid box there should be an accident book and if 10 or more people are employed on the same premises then keeping an accident book is compulsory.

Many accidents will be minor but sometimes an accident that appears trivial at the time, will develop into a more serious condition later. The injury may cause pain, loss of earnings and even make it impossible for the employee to carry on in the same employment. The employee may decide to seek compensation and if this is the case the accident book will provide crucial evidence. Therefore it must be completed as soon as possible. If the person who has had the accident is too badly injured, then it should be filled in on their behalf. The employer must investigate the cause of the accident and if they find anything different record it on the form. If an accident leads to the employee being absent from work for three days or more then the employer has to report the accident to the Environmental Health Department or if a local government organization the health and safety executive. The accident forms are confidential and must be kept for at least three years. Accident books can be designed by the organization or purchased from HMSO, PO Box 276, London SW8 5DT. Figure 1.5 shows a page from an accident book (the information can vary depending on the organization).

► EQUIPMENT FAULTS

From time to time equipment will develop faults, particularly items such as photocopier, typewriter, computer, printer, automatic mailing equipment. If a piece of office equipment is not functioning then this could create many problems, particularly if there is no back-up equipment. It is important that you maintain the equipment properly and do not abuse it. You can regularly clean equipment yourself using special cleaning materials available from most office equipment suppliers. For hygienic reasons it is important to clean the telephone handset regularly with an anti-bacterial wipe. Some organizations choose to pay to have their equipment regularly cleaned and maintained by the suppliers or contract cleaners.

ACCIDENT BOOK

NAME OF PERSON WHO HAD THE ACCIDENT ....

HOME ADDRESS ....

....

OCCUPATION ....

WHERE DID THE ACCIDENT HAPPEN? ....

....

DATE .... TIME ....

HOW DID THE ACCIDENT HAPPEN? ....

....

....

ACTION TAKEN ....

....

....

Signature .... Employer's signature ....

If you did not have the accident yourself but are completing the details, fill in this section.

NAME ....

HOME ADDRESS ....

....

OCCUPATION ....

Figure 1.5 *A page from an accident book*

Should a fault occur, then first consult your instruction manual. It may be something very simple which you can rectify yourself. If not, follow the organization's procedure for reporting faults. Inform your supervisor or technician, if you have one, or contact the supplier/manufacturer. It is important when you receive a new piece of equipment to keep the **contact telephone number** for service/assistance in a safe place, preferably in your filing system under 'equipment'.

> **REMEMBER!** *Never attempt to repair a piece of equipment yourself without seeking permission from your supervisor/boss.*

BUSINESS COMMUNICATIONS AND RELATIONSHIPS

► WRITTEN COMMUNICATIONS

Supplying information in written form is one of the major ways that organizations communicate. The two main advantages of written communication in business are:

1 It is a permanent record that can be retained.

2 The information can be viewed at leisure.

If you are asked to present a piece of information, you must firstly consider which method would be most effective.

> *THINK!* *Would a brief note suffice? What about a memorandum? Would a letter be more professional? Would the information be easier to understand in diagram form, eg a pie chart or organization chart? Is a full report required to explain the situation thoroughly? Would a notice have more impact than a memorandum?*

It is important that any piece of written communication is well presented, well structured and free from spelling/punctuation errors, as this communication may be the first impression a customer/client receives of your organization.

Finding out information

Before writing anything, prepare your facts: ensure you have the correct information and if you are not sure, check. Use reference sources. Table 2.1 is a guide to gathering information. For any other kind of information not listed in the table, it is suggested that you consult your reference library, or make direct contact with the appropriate business or department concerned, eg travel agent, Department of Social Security.

Table 2.1   Information guide

Reference sources	Information required	Obtain from
Company records	Statistical information	Company secretary
Travel timetables	Times of departure and arrival for air/sea/rail/coach travel	Travel agents Railway station Airport, etc.
Phone book	Telephone numbers and addresses	British Telecom Library
Yellow Pages	Business addresses and telephone numbers: classified under trade or profession, eg restaurants, dentists	British Telecom Library
Fax directory Telex directory	Fax and Telex numbers	British Telecom Library
AA and RAC handbook	Road maps, road distances and accommodation	The AA/RAC Library
Dictionary	Meanings of words and spellings	Stationers Book shops Library Computer packages
Roget's Thesaurus	Alternative words with the same meaning	Book shops Libraries Computer package
Whitaker's Almanack	General information on all countries of the world	Book shops Libraries
Who's Who	Information on famous people in Britain	Book shops Libraries
UK Kompass	Information about companies and the products/services they offer. Names of directors and number of employees	Subscription Library Chamber of Commerce
The Post Office Guide	Information on all services offered by the Post Office	Post Office Library

Table 2.1   (Cont'd)

Reference sources	Information required	Obtain from
Teletext	General information, share prices, weather and travel information, tourist exchange rates, world clock, company reports	ITV (Oracle) BBC (Ceefax)
Viewdata (Prestel) Interactive, ie as well as viewing the user can actually book the hotel by using the keyboard to give instructions	More business related information, eg bank services, car hire, hotel bookings	Special equipment required and subscription to British Telecom Some libraries
Microfiche	Any information may be microfilmed to save space. By microfilming, an A4 page will be reduced to the size of a postage stamp. The information is then enlarged on a special screen for viewing. Telephone directories now available on microfiche	The equipment for viewing microfiche is now available in most main libraries and also in some offices

Letter writing

This is used as a formal means of communication and when communicating with people outside your organization.

It is vitally important that the presentation, tone and content of a letter are correct, as it will give the recipient an impression of your organization. Many companies have their own 'house style' of letter layout, and if so, this should be followed. However, if you are not given any instruction on presentation of letters, follow the example of a business letter given in Figure 2.1.

Tips on letter writing

- Always type the date in full, eg 6 May 199*: do not abbreviate to 6/5/9*.
- Our ref. usually consists of the writer's and the typist's initials, plus any other reference number the company may use.

16

SHEPPERTON INDUSTRIES PLC

SHEPPERTON HOUSE
APPELTON INDUSTRIAL ESTATE   WA3 2BP

Our Ref: BW/sk
Your Ref:

18th March 199*

Mrs A E Jackson
15 Cranford Street
Morton
Manchester
M30 9PW

Dear Mrs Jackson

VACANCY FOR CANTEEN SUPERVISOR

Thank you for your letter applying for the above vacancy.

Our Catering Manager, Mr J Hunt, would like to meet you on Friday 29th
March 199* to discuss this position further. Please report to Reception at
2.30pm. A map is enclosed to help you find our premises. Any travelling
expenses that you incur will be reimbursed, so do retain your travel ticket
or record your car mileage.

If you are unable to attend, please let me know at your earliest
convenience.

Yours sincerely

BRENDA WRAGG (Miss)
Personnel Manager

Enc

Figure 2.1 *Business letter*

- Only insert 'your ref.' if you are replying to a piece of correspondence, where they have used a reference.
- If you commence with the formal salutation: Dear Sir, Dear Sirs, Dear Madam, then use the complimentary close: Yours faithfully. If you commence with the salutation: Dear (name), then use the complimentary close: Yours sincerely.
- In general aim for three paragraphs:
  - an introduction: this may be thanking them for their letter;
  - purpose of the letter;
  - conclusion.
  See Figure 2.1.
- Check your letter carefully: **we all make mistakes**. Use a dictionary or spell-check on your word processing package, or perhaps ask a colleague to check it for you.

> **REMEMBER!** It is usual to take a copy for future reference.

Memoranda

A memorandum (plural: memoranda) is used to convey information within an organization.

Though used internally it is still important to structure a memorandum, often abbreviated to memo, carefully, so that it reads clearly. You may be sending a memo to a more senior member of staff and so it is important to create a good impression. Very often it is better to write a memo, rather than scribble a note, as the information is less likely to get misplaced. Organizations often use pre-printed memo forms, but if not follow the examples shown in Figures 2.2 and 2.3.

Tips on writing memos

- As shown in the examples, memos should be concise and to the point, but there is no limit on length. Some memos may be more than one page of A4.
- No letter headed paper needed as used internally.
- No inside address required.
- No salutation such as 'Dear Sir' required.
- No complimentary close such as 'Yours faithfully' required.
- Memos do not need to be signed.
- State the name and position/department of the person the memo is going to and the person it is from.

- It is helpful to give a heading to the memo, so that the recipient can see immediately what it is about.

MEMORANDUM

FROM: Brenda Wragg   Ref: BAW/SK
      Personnel Manager

TO: Mr J Hunt   DATE: 18th March 199*
      Catering Manager

VACANCY FOR CANTEEN SUPERVISOR

This is to confirm that I have invited Mrs A E Jackson to meet you regarding the above position on Friday 29th March 199* at 2.30 pm. Reception will inform you when she arrives. I will arrange for a copy of her application letter to be sent to you.

- -

Figure 2.2 *Example of a memo from manager to manager*

MEMORANDUM

FROM: Brenda Wragg   Ref: BAW/SK
      Personnel Manager

TO: Mrs C Roberts   DATE: 18th March 199*
      Receptionist

Please note that Mrs A E Jackson will be attending for an interview with Mr J Hunt, Catering Manager, on Friday 29th March 199* at 2.30 pm. Please inform Mr Hunt when she arrives and reimburse her travelling expenses.

- -

Figure 2.3 *Example of a memo from manager to receptionist*

Reports

These are used to convey findings, following a request for information.

It is unlikely that you will be asked to write a formal report yourself, but you may be asked to present information prepared by a more senior employee in

19

1. HEADING   REPORT ON WORK PLACEMENT
                                     AT ......
                           FROM ....   TO ....

2. TERMS OF REFERENCE: This report has been requested by .... and
is to be submitted by ....(date).

3. METHOD OF INQUIRY: The period of work placement was undertaken at
.... between the following dates ....
During this time I observed, listened, and asked questions in order to fin
out the details listed in the Findings section of this report.

4. FINDINGS: (List here the departments worked in, the role of each
department and the administrative functions undertaken)

5. CONCLUSION: (Was your work placement beneficial?   What did you enjoy
or not enjoy?)

6. RECOMMENDATIONS: (Write here any recommendations you have for work
placement. Was the placement too long or short? Was your supervision
satisfactory?)

7. SIGNATURE ....

8. DATE ....

Figure 2.4 *An example of how a formal report may be written on work placement*

this style. In a formal report the material is presented in a specific format,
using headings and subheadings, so that it is easy to find a particular section
without having to read the whole report. Figure 2.4 is an example of a formal
report to be prepared on a student's experiences of work placement. The same
headings would be used for any formal report. Formal reports involve
investigation, as you will see from the nature of the headings.

Envelopes

To ensure confidentiality, most pieces of correspondence, including memoranda, will be placed in an envelope. It is important not to spoil the image of
your letter by sending it in a poorly prepared envelope. It also helps the Post
Office and speeds the delivery if the address is clearly and correctly written.

Firstly select an envelope that is a suitable size and address it as shown in Figure 2.5. Fold the correspondence carefully and prepare for mailing (see mailing section).

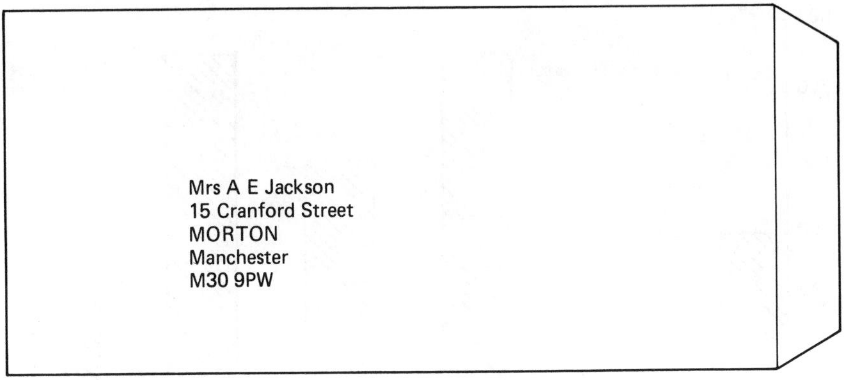

Mrs A E Jackson
15 Cranford Street
MORTON
Manchester
M30 9PW

Figure 2.5 *Addressing an envelope*

Diagrams

These are used to present figures and to create more interest.

It is often more effective to present figures in diagram form. Imagine you are given the following information to present:

Sales of light bulbs for January 1992 (to nearest thousand)
Head Office 500 000
London 300 000
Birmingham 750 000
Bristol 600 000
Edinburgh 750 000
Manchester 400 000

How could you present the information clearly and effectively?

THINK *about: a bar chart, a line graph, a pie chart, a pictogram, tabulation.*

Bar chart

A bar chart could be drawn up quite simply to provide the information as shown in Figure 2.6. It is important to give the chart a heading and label the axes clearly or the information will not be meaningful.

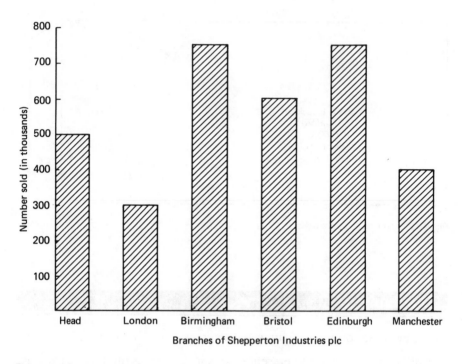

Figure 2.6 *Bar chart to show the sale of light bulbs for January 199**

Line graph

A line graph would not be suitable for presenting this information, as this type of graph is more appropriate for showing information over a period of time. Line graphs are also excellent for comparing figures. There are too many depots in the original information to illustrate clearly, but a line graph would be suitable for showing the sale of light bulbs for one or more depots over several months. This is illustrated in Figure 2.7.

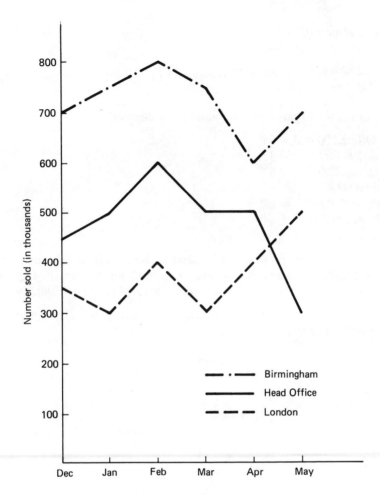

Figure 2.7 *Line graph to show the sale of light bulbs over a six-month period*

Pie chart

A pie chart would be appropriate (see Figure 2.8), but is more difficult to calculate if prepared accurately. The figures have to be changed into degrees, so that each item will be shown as a proportion of the circle. To do this you must first know that there are 360 degrees in a circle. Then use the following formula:

$$\frac{\text{No. of degrees in circle}}{\text{The sum of all the figures to be entered in pie chart}} \times \text{Each figure}$$

Example: *Head Office*

$$\frac{360}{3\ 300\ 000} \times 500\ 000 = 54 = 55 \text{ (rounded up)}$$

Use a protractor to mark out the number of degrees.

Head Office 500 000 = 55°
London 300 000   = 32°
Birmingham 750 000   = 82°
Bristol 600 000   = 65°
Edinburgh 750 000   = 82°
Manchester 400 000   = 44°
              Total = 360°

Many people do not prepare a pie chart as accurately as this, and would simply estimate the segments to give an overall impression. If a graphics package on a computer is used, then this will simplify the calculations.

With a pie chart it is important to label each segment clearly. It is often easier to interpret if you write the figures on each segment.

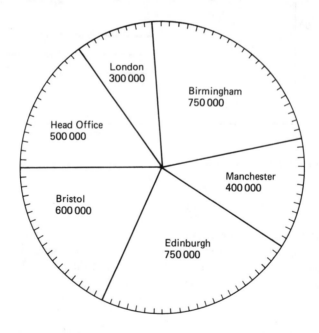

Figure 2.8 *Pie chart to show the sale of light bulbs for January 199* (to nearest thousand)*

Pictogram

A pictogram could be used to represent this information quite simply and effectively, provided one picture symbol was used to represent a large number of items, ie one picture symbol = one hundred thousand light bulbs, this must be clearly stated to avoid confusion.

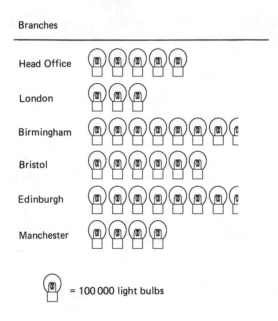

= 100 000 light bulbs

Figure 2.9 *Pictogram to show the sale of light bulbs for January 199* (to nearest thousand)*

Tabulation

A tabulation would be the clearest way to show the actual figures, but again it would be more suitable if we were to show the information over a longer period of time, ie the figures for February, March, and April in addition to January, so that they could be compared. Figure 2.10 is an example of a simple tabulation.

There are many other forms of written communication to convey more precise information, many of which you will read about in other sections of this book, eg the organization charts shown in Section 1, notices, telephone messages, travel itineraries, agendas, order forms, invoices. Please refer to the Index.

Sales of light bulbs January 199*					
Head Office	London	B'ham	Bristol	Edin.	Manchester
500 000	300 000	750 000	600 000	750 000	400 000

Figure 2.10 *Tabulation to show actual sales figures for January 199**

Occasionally you may feel that a simple handwritten note would suffice: if so then make sure you include the date, the name of the person that the note is intended for and your name. Otherwise notes can be meaningless and easily lost.

► VERBAL COMMUNICATIONS

Speaking to people either face to face or over the telephone is an essential means of communication for any organization. Just imagine how difficult it would be for you personally to survive without being able to communicate verbally. For an organization the advantage of this form of communication is that the response is immediate and therefore business matters can be sorted out very quickly.

When working in an office you will almost certainly have to make and receive telephone calls, and receive occasional visitors. However, you may prefer to be in the front line, dealing with customers/clients as a:

- Receptionist.
- Telephonist operating the switchboard.
- Sales administrator.

THINK! The impression you give could either lose or create business, so be polite, helpful and professional. Remember a smile not only helps the caller but makes you feel better and is reflected in your voice.

Making and receiving telephone calls

Figures 2.11, 2.12 and 2.13 are guidelines for dealing with incoming and outgoing telephone calls and their relevant messages.

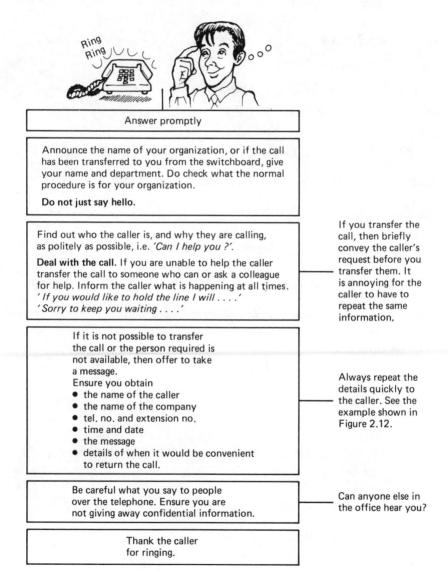

Answer promptly

Announce the name of your organization, or if the call has been transferred to you from the switchboard, give your name and department. Do check what the normal procedure is for your organization.

Do not just say hello.

Find out who the caller is, and why they are calling, as politely as possible, i.e. *'Can I help you ?'.*

Deal with the call. If you are unable to help the caller transfer the call to someone who can or ask a colleague for help. Inform the caller what is happening at all times. *'If you would like to hold the line I will . . . .'* *'Sorry to keep you waiting . . . .'*

If you transfer the call, then briefly convey the caller's request before you transfer them. It is annoying for the caller to have to repeat the same information.

If it is not possible to transfer the call or the person required is not available, then offer to take a message.
Ensure you obtain
● the name of the caller
● the name of the company
● tel. no. and extension no.
● time and date
● the message
● details of when it would be convenient to return the call.

Always repeat the details quickly to the caller. See the example shown in Figure 2.12.

Be careful what you say to people over the telephone. Ensure you are not giving away confidential information.

Can anyone else in the office hear you?

Thank the caller for ringing.

Figure 2.11 *Dealing with incoming telephone calls*

27

TELEPHONE MESSAGE FORM

DATE: .20.-3.-9*............ TIME: ....3.15 pm............

FOR: ..Brenda..Wragg.....

FROM: ..Mrs..Jackson...... ORGANIZATION: .....⌐...............

TEL: ..061-709-2164....... EXT ...⌐............

MESSAGE: Mrs Jackson phoned regarding her appt
with Mr Hunt for the canteen supervisor vacancy.
Unfortunately 2.30pm on 29 March is inconvenient
as her son has a hospital appt at this time.
Would it be possible for her to come in the
morning? She will phone you again tomorrow
afternoon.

Taken by: .S. Kennedy......

Figure 2.12 *Telephone message form*

Do you know what you are phoning about?
Gather all relevant information together.
Do not waste time and money by making
unnecessary calls and having to find out
information while on the line.

Time of day
Is the call urgent? If not wait until
it is cheaper rate.

Do you know the telephone number?
Refer to:
- letter headed stationery
- The Phone Book
- Directory Enquiries.
Write the telephone number down.

Dial the telephone number.
Announce who you are and who you wish
to speak to.
Leave a message if they are unavailable.

Ringing tone: repeated
burr burr
Engaged tone: repeated
single tone
Number unobtainable: steady tone

Speak clearly. Be polite, even if you
are complaining.

Be careful what you say to
people and what information you
disclose. Remember confidentiality.

Figure 2.13 *Dealing with outgoing telephone calls*

Remember the professional image you wish to create. Look at Figure 2.14(a). Do you use these expressions? They are fine when speaking to a friend but in the office be professional: think about telephone technique and, as in Figure 2.14(b), use helpful, clearly understood expressions.

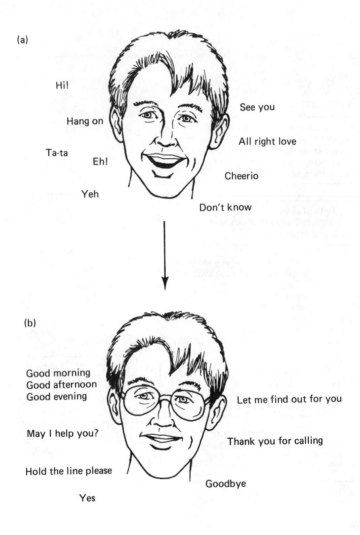

Figure 2.14 *Telephone technique: (a) speaking to a friend; (b) remember the professional image*

It often creates a good impression to refer to the caller's name if known or add Sir/Madam to certain phrases, ie 'Thank you for calling Sir', 'Let me find out for you Mr Brown'. Unless you are told otherwise, use the caller's surname.

Using the telephone directory

If you do not know the telephone number, then there are various directories available to help you.

The Phone Book

Each Phone Book covers a different area. All telephone users receive a local Phone Book, which has the following:

- Information on local services, eg hospitals, transport.
- A list of subscribers in the area, and their telephone numbers, in alphabetical order by surname.
- Dialling codes.

  Note:
  To make a call in your own exchange area, you do not need a code.
  To make a call to another exchange within your local area, dial the code given in the local call section and then the number.
  To make a call outside your local area, dial the national code then the number.
  To make a call abroad, dial the international code then the number.

Your Phone Book will give you all this information. International dialling codes are also given in the reference section of the phone book.

- Details of British Telecom services.

Yellow Pages

These are trade directories. Each telephone user receives a local Yellow Pages. Every business in the area is listed in alphabetical order of their profession or occupation. Some choose to buy additional advertising space.

Business Pages

There are seven Business Pages directories covering: Yorkshire and North East; West Pennines; West Midlands; London; East Midlands; Central Southern; Bristol and South Wales. The directories give information on businesses, professional bodies and trading associations that are specifically aimed at being of interest to business people rather than the consumer.

Local and national calls

The tables on these pages give examples of the approximate cost of various dialled calls in each charge band. Prices depend on the call unit fee, the length of your call, the time of day that you make your call and where you are calling.

Standard call unit fee 4.2p (4.935p including VAT)

Type of call and charge band	Cheap rate Mon-Fri 6pm-8am All weekend (note 1)		
	1 min	3 mins	5 mins
Local calls (L)	5p	5p	10p
National calls up to 56.4km* outside local call area – (a)	5p	15p	20p
National calls over 56.4km* connected over low cost routes – (b1)	10p	20p	30p
National calls over 56.4km*, calls to the Channel Islands and Isle of Man – (b)	10p	25p	40p
Calls to mobile telephones 0860 nos, 0831 nos and some 0836 nos, 0850 nos (notes 2 & 3) and 0881 nos – (m)	30p	79p	£1.34
Calls to Callstream service 0898, 0839, 08364 nos – (p 1)	40p	£1.09	£1.83

*Approximately 35 miles

0800 & 0345 CALLS

If a number begins 0800 the call is **FREE** to you and if it begins 0345, you'll only be charged at **LOCAL CALL RATES** – no matter where you're calling from in the UK.

Note 1: *Normal charges apply on all bank holidays except Christmas Day, Boxing Day and New Year's Day when the cheap rate period is extended throughout the day.*

Note 2: *Calls to some numbers beginning 0836 are charged at a lower rate.*

Note 3: *Calls will also be chargeable when they are answered by Cellular networks on the called number's behalf – including recorded announcements.*

Local and national calls

In these examples we have used the standard call unit fee of 4.2p (4.935p inc VAT). But remember, if you use up enough units per quarter, then the fee will vary (see pages 3 & 4). All examples include VAT at 17½%.

Standard rate Mon-Fri 8am-9am and 1pm-6pm			Peak rate Mon-Fri 9am-1pm		
1 min	3 mins	5 mins	1 min	3 mins	5 mins
5p	15p	20p	5p	20p	30p
10p	25p	45p	10p	35p	60p
10p	30p	50p	15p	40p	65p
15p	40p	60p	20p	50p	79p
40p	£1.19	£1.98	40p	£1.19	£1.98
50p	£1.49	£2.42	50p	£1.49	£2.42

FREEFONE CALLS

A FreeFone call is **FREE** to you. Simply dial 100 and ask the operator to put you through to the FreeFone Name you require.

DIRECTORY ENQUIRY CALLS

Each call to Directory Enquiries is charged at 9 units at the prevailing call unit fee (see pages 3 & 4). Each call allows customers to request a search for up to two telephone numbers.

Figure 2.15 Extract from British Telecom inland call charges leaflet

If you cannot find the telephone number in your directory or elsewhere then phone directory enquiries: 192, but remember there is now a charge for this enquiry. Have a pencil and paper ready to take down the number.

Telephone charges

You can save a great deal of money for your organization by understanding how telephone calls are costed.

Some organizations like you to log all outgoing telephone calls and estimate the cost.

Calls within the United Kingdom are costed by British Telecom, depending on the time of day that you make your call and on where you are calling. Calls are placed in charge bands, depending on distance (L = local call, a = calls up to approximately 35 miles, b = calls over 35 miles and b1 = calls over 35 miles on frequently used routes). Your Phone Book will tell you the charge band for the town you are calling. Figure 2.15 gives examples of the approximate cost.

International calls are again costed by British Telecom according to the time of day and the country's charge band. There are 13 charge bands for international calls. As a comparison, charge band 1 would include countries such as Belgium, Italy, Denmark, Germany, Gibraltar, Greece, Spain, Switzerland, and the approximate cost would be as shown in Figure 2.16.

Charge band	Rate	Average per minute		5-minute call		10-minute call	
		ex. VAT	inc. VAT	ex. VAT	inc. VAT	ex. VAT	inc. VAT
1	Cheap rate	£0.28	£0.33	£1.39	£1.63	£2.73	£3.21
	Standard rate	£0.34	£0.39	£1.68	£1.98	£3.32	£3.90

Figure 2.16 *International calls band 1*

Charge band 12 would include such countries as Bangladesh, India, Pakistan, Sri Lanka and the approximate cost is shown in Figure 2.17.

12	Cheap rate	£1.08	£1.27	£5.42	£6.37	£10.80	£12.69
	Standard rate	£1.14	£1.34	£5.67	£6.67	£11.34	£13.33

Figure 2.17 *International calls band 12*

Switchboard

The switchboard is the piece of equipment that connects your organization to the telephone exchange. Usually switchboards have more than one incoming line, so that several calls can be handled at once. A switchboard will also have a number of internal extensions to transfer the calls to. Switchboards used to be very large and cumbersome and require specific training, but now the majority are computerized and automatic, which means that though incoming calls will come through the switchboard, outgoing calls can be made from extensions direct without the operator's help.

Some organizations do not have a switchboard and calls are routed to any available telephone, which means that you could be answering incoming calls on behalf of the organization, even though you are not the switchboard operator.

There are many different telephone systems to cope with companies' individual needs. Figures 2.18, 2.19, 2.20 and 2.21 are examples of various phone systems available from British Telecom, and their special features.

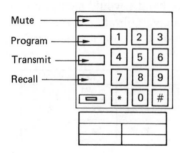

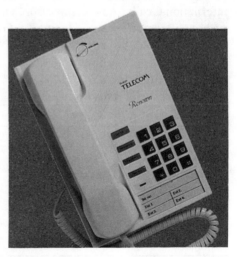

This telephone has one incoming telephone line that can be linked to four extensions. It therefore lets you answer and redirect calls to appropriate extensions. Callers can be placed on hold. External calls can be dialled direct from any extension. There is an external line-in-use light to show whether someone else is using the line.

Figure 2.18 *Renown*

This telephone can handle one or two incoming lines and up to four extensions. It is a key system, which means that each phone linked to it acts as a mini-switchboard, so that anyone can answer incoming calls and act as operator. This can be used in conjunction with the main switchboard as a departmental system.

Figure 2.19 *Ambassador Ess*

This key and lamp console sits alongside each extension phone and allows all employees to answer incoming calls and redirect calls if necessary at the touch of a couple of buttons. This saves the caller having to wait for the switchboard operator to answer calls. The system may have 8 lines/8 extensions or 16 lines/ extensions. It is very useful for any organization that has a number of employees able to offer help and expertise to callers, e.g. help lines, telephone sales.

Figure 2.20 *Navigator*

Octara can handle up to 10 lines and up to 32 extensions. This telephone system also features music on hold, a public address system, paging and loudspeaker operation.

Figure 2.21 *Octara 32X*

As a switchboard operator you will need to have:

● A good knowledge of the organization and the role of people/ departments.
● A pleasant voice.
● Patience to deal with difficult customers/clients.
● A good telephone technique.
● The ability to keep calm under pressure.

The switchboard operator may also be the receptionist.

Telephone answering machines

Many organizations now choose to have a telephone answering machine, so that should no one be available to answer the telephone, the caller can always leave a message. This is particularly useful out-of-hours, during holidays and at lunch times. There are various types of telephone answering machines and it is important to refer to the manufacturer's instruction manual on how to operate the equipment.

Most telephone answering machines have the following features:

● Play a message to incoming callers.
● Record incoming messages.
● Indicate when a message has been received.

- Play, rewind and fast forward feature.
- Message erase.

It is important that the message you record for incoming callers is short, but informative. You may change the message as often as you wish. Here is an example of a message.

'Hello, this is Foss Chemicals. I am sorry there is no one available to take your call personally, but if you would like to leave your name and telephone number, together with any message, your call will be returned as soon as possible. Please start speaking after the long tone.'

When you return to the office, check immediately if any messages have been left. Rewind and play the tape and transcribe the messages on to a telephone message form as quickly as possible. See Section 2, page 28. Rewind and replay the message as necessary. Either deal with the call yourself or pass the message on to the appropriate person. Ensure that you record the date and time when you transcribed the message.

Glossary of telephone terms

Abbreviated dialling Regularly dialled numbers can be given abbreviated codes for faster dialling.

Automatic redialling If the number you are trying to reach is engaged, the telephone system will repeat the number until it is successful.

Call divert Incoming calls may be diverted to another telephone number. The caller will hear the message 'please hold the line, your call is being diverted'.

Conference call The ability to set up a three-way conversation between one outside caller and two or more people on internal extensions.

Freefone When organizations offer a telephone number to ring as Freefone 8412, the customer can dial the operator and be connected to that organization free of charge. The organization is then charged for the price of the call plus a charge for the service.

Mobile phone (cell phone) A phone that can be carried by a person or in a vehicle.

Radio pager A small pocket-size piece of equipment that allows the holder to be bleeped anywhere in the UK. This indicates that someone wishes to contact you and it is important to telephone back to your base. Many pagers now give a written message (Figure 2.22).

Pagers are available with a silent vibrating alert that lets you know you're wanted without making a sound. Invaluable in noisy environments or when a bleep could be intrusive.

Figure 2.22 *Example of a pager that will give a written message*

Secrecy button By pressing the secrecy button on a phone, the caller would not be able to hear what you were saying. The same thing could happen by putting the caller on **hold**.

Add below any notes that you would like to make on telephone services.

RECEPTION WORK

As a receptionist you have a very special role, for the initial impression that a customer/client receives of an organization is from the receptionist and the reception area. Recall any reception areas that you have been to, such as:

- Your doctor's surgery.
- Local hospital.
- Hotels.
- Colleges.
- Local companies.

What impression did you receive of the organization? Did the receptionist put you at ease?

The reception area

If you were able to design a reception area then consideration would have to be given to the image that you wanted to create. The company may wish to appear hi-tech with modern furniture, in coordinated colours, eg red and grey, yellow and black, or it may wish to give a more traditional image, for example a solicitors' practice may prefer antique furniture and leather chairs. A dentist may wish his reception area to be as relaxing as possible with easy chairs, flowered wallpaper and soft music playing. A hotel may want to give a feeling of warmth, luxury and relaxation. Whatever the furniture and fittings a reception area must:

1 Provide a comfortable waiting area.

2 Be clean and tidy.

Many receptionists are not fortunate enough to design the area themselves, but it may be possible to enhance the environment with the addition of:

- Pictures.
- Houseplants and flowers.
- Magazines.
- Window blinds.
- Possibly a fish tank.

Rearranging the furniture can also make a big difference.

> **IMPORTANT**   Do discuss with your supervisor and colleagues before making any changes.

The receptionist

Do you have to be young, female and beautiful to be a good receptionist? No: in fact this may not be the image the organization wishes to give. You must be professional and the qualities featured in Figure 2.23 are most important in order to create the right impression.

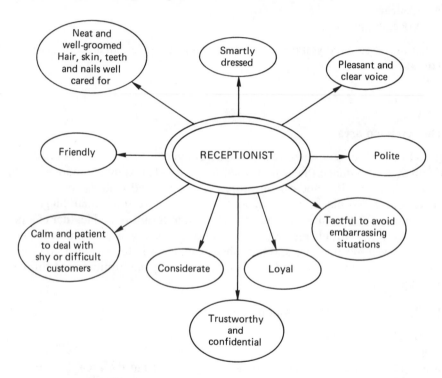

Figure 2.23 *The receptionist*

Reception duties

As a receptionist you will probably be given a job description or told the jobs you are expected to do. You may be solely a receptionist, or you may also be responsible for the switchboard, handling mail, typing, filing, etc. The following are duties that the majority of receptionists would be expected to perform.

1 Receiving customers/clients. You may have to greet customers/clients even if you are not working as the receptionist. The following rules apply.

   a Greet visitors promptly. If you are unable to speak to them immediately (perhaps you are on the telephone or dealing with another visitor) then acknowledge their presence with a smile.

   b Be courteous. Remember that they are visitors and should be treated with respect. Smile and be polite.

   c Identify their needs. 'Good morning, may I help you'. Take their name and address: you may be offered a business card.

   d Deal with the visitor yourself or summon appropriate personnel.

   e Ask the visitor to take a seat while you contact the appropriate personnel by telephone or loud speaker, ie 'Mr Brown please report to reception'.

   f Inform the visitor what is happening and apologize if you have to keep them waiting.

   g Offer refreshments if appropriate.

   h Direct the visitor to their destination or arrange for them to be escorted.

   i If the caller is unexpected and no one is available to see them, explain the situation and arrange a future appointment or take a message. It may be that the caller's query could be dealt with by a telephone call or a letter, thus saving everybody's time.

   j Be careful about the information you disclose to the visitor. Remember confidentiality.

2 Keeping records. This can be done in several ways, and you may be expected to look after any or all of the following books.

   a The appointments book. You may be asked to keep the appointments book and make all appointments for customers/clients (see Figure 2.24). In some organizations you will simply be informed by other personnel about the visitors they are expecting each day.

APPOINTMENTS BOOK

Date ....

Time of appt.	Name	Company	To see	Special instructions

Figure 2.24 *A page from an appointments book*

b The visitors book/register. Many organizations keep a record of all visitors (Figure 2.25). This is useful for:

(i) knowing exactly who is on the premises, particularly in case of fire or security problems;

(ii) handling any incoming calls for visitors;

(iii) showing which staff are engaged;

(iv) future reference, eg a health and leisure club may send out advertisement literature to all visitors.

c The staff 'in and out' book. Staff sign in and out so that you know which personnel are on the premises.

3 Maintaining the reception area. As a receptionist it will be your duty to maintain the area and ensure that with the help of caretakers and cleaners it is always kept clean and tidy. Use the following checklist to ensure that you carry out your duties properly.

.... Ashtrays — empty.

.... Magazines — relevant and up to date, limit the number you have.

.... Plants — watered.

.... Flowers — fresh, change water if necessary.

.... Notices — displayed clearly, not cluttered, out-of-date notices removed, ensure notices are appropriate.

VISITORS BOOK

Date	Time of arrival	Name	Company	To see	Signature	Time of departure

Note: Depending on the organization, an additional column may be added to record the visitor's pass number or car registration number.

Figure 2.25 *A page from a visitors book*

43

.... Display material — any displays advertising the services of the organization are relevant and up to date. (You do not wish to advertise products that are no longer manufactured.)

.... Floor coverings — well maintained to prevent accidents. Not wet and slippery. Request floor mat if necessary.

.... Direction signs — accurate and prominent.

.... Calendar (date) correct.

.... Clock accurate.

.... Lighting/heating — report any problems.

.... Furniture and fittings — report any problems, particularly if unsafe.

.... First-aid box — clearly labelled and fully equipped.

.... Fire notices/equipment — prominent. Ensure you know the fire procedure.

4 Order stationery and supplies as required for reception. See Section 5.

5 Receive parcels and mail for distribution to relevant departments/ personnel. See Section 4.

6 Operate the switchboard.

7 Implement the organization's security procedure.

8 Take responsibility for health and safety within the reception area and maintain the first-aid box.

9 Promote the organization by issuing advertisement literature or information if appropriate.

Security procedures

Some organizations will be very security conscious when receiving visitors, others less so. It is important to check on the policy of the organization if you are not told what to do. The following policies may be implemented to ensure that theft, damage to premises and injury to personnel are avoided.

Visitors' passes

As well as entering the details of the visitor in the visitors book, each visitor is issued with a pass or badge that is usually returned to reception on departure. This indicates to other personnel that the person is a visitor who has been checked in at reception and not just wandered into the building. It is also a way of checking that all visitors have left the premises at the end of the day.

Appointments

Many organizations refuse to see callers without a prior arranged appointment. This prevents casual callers.

Proof of identity

In top secrecy establishments, proof of identity may be requested by the receptionist.

Escorting visitors

All visitors are escorted to their destination and no visitors are allowed to wander around the building by themselves.

Baggage

In some organizations baggage is checked, left at reception or left with security.

> **IMPORTANT** *Should you suspect any problems then contact your supervisor, security or the police.*

Emergency situations

Familiarize yourself with the organization's procedure for dealing with the following:

- fire
- bomb scares
- accidents.

As receptionist/switchboard operator you may be the person who has to summon the emergency services and sound the alarm: **check on this**.

As receptionist you will almost certainly be responsible for evacuating the reception area and ensuring that you escort any visitors in reception to the appropriate assembly area. **If you have to evacuate, make sure you take the visitors book with you**, to check who is on the premises. Close the doors and see that no one enters the building.

You may also be responsible for dealing with any medical emergencies in the reception area. You may have a first-aid certificate, but even so use your common sense. Summon trained medical help if you have medical staff on the premises. Give simple first-aid if appropriate or dial 999 for an ambulance if the situation is obviously serious.

Tips on reception work

- Check the organization's policy on dealing with visitors.
- Ensure that you have an organization chart.
- An internal telephone list is essential.
- Familiarize yourself with the local area, ie car parks, hotels.
- Retain business cards and keep in an alphabetical index under the firm's name for future reference.
- Use the visitor's name where appropriate.
- If the caller leaves a message, write it down immediately and make sure it reaches the right person as soon as possible.

Glossary of terms

Confidentiality   When working for an organization there will be many things that you learn about as an employee which should be kept secret from other employees, visitors or people outside the organization. For example, a company may not wish competitors to know the selling price of goods, how the goods are made or carriage charges. You may be involved with personnel problems, which are personal, eg regarding illness, or disciplinary procedure, that should be kept private. You must use common sense and think before you disclose information.

> **THINK!**   *If you are discussing anything personal or confidential, ensure that your conversation is not overheard. If you are writing a confidential letter, make sure that it is not left around for people to see. If confidential material is on your VDU check that it cannot be read by others.*

Etiquette   In business a certain standard of professional behaviour is expected and this is discussed further in the next section. For example, you would not call the visitor a name that may cause offence, eg 'mate'.

Loyalty   To be a good employee, loyalty to the organization is essential and this is particularly important when dealing with customers/clients. This means that you would support the organization whatever your personal feelings and not discourage customers by making negative remarks.

Tact   Being tactful is a very important quality for any office workers, but particularly for the receptionist. A receptionist may find it necessary to adapt a situation to avoid friction and to save causing offence. For example, if a colleague refuses to see a visitor then rather than saying to the visitor: 'Mr Brown does not wish to see you', which may cause offence, suggest that another member of staff may be more suitable to deal with the matter or that they leave a message or write to Mr Brown as he is unavailable at present.

▶ BUSINESS RELATIONSHIPS

Working in an office you will almost certainly have to maintain good business (working) relationships when dealing with other staff, other organizations, customers/clients.

Creating good business relationships really depends upon your 'people skills', how well you relate and deal with superiors, colleagues and customers. This involves listening, interpreting body language and responding appropriately. Even the expression on a person's face can tell you whether they are happy, annoyed, confused, etc, and this often provides a warning signal before a difficult situation arises.

Working with colleagues

To create a good **working relationship** with colleagues, you must first understand:

1   The structure of the organization and how you fit in to that structure.

2   Who you are responsible to and what your role is.

Your attitude will be very important in creating the right relationships and the following guidelines are suggested.

- Be helpful to others, whether superiors or juniors.
- Be willing to carry out your job to the best of your ability.
- Act promptly and thoroughly in carrying out any requests, so that people trust you to do the job properly.
- Be polite when asking for assistance. Unless it is urgent wait until the person required is free.
- Offer help to others if you are not busy and they are. Nothing causes more friction between staff than an uneven workload. In return they may then help you when the situation is reversed.

- Be cooperative even when busy.
- Be courteous to everyone, regardless of position, for when you are new to an organization it is difficult to know who is who and you do not wish to upset any members of staff.

> **THINK!** It is accepted that you will be more friendly with a close colleague than you will be with your supervisor or manager. Take things slowly and do not become too familiar at first. Refer to seniors by their full title, ie Mr Kennedy, unless they ask you to address them differently.

There will be occasions when you disagree with colleagues and friction arises (Figure 2.26). Try to resolve your differences as amicably and quickly as possible, even if you are the one who has to offer the apology: remember that you are now in a working environment and in administration teamwork is essential. Should the problem not be resolved then discuss it with your supervisor.

Figure 2.26 *Colleagues can agree and disagree!*

Customers/clients/outside agencies

When dealing with people outside the organization, rather than building up a working relationship, you are trying to create and maintain a **professional relationship**. We have discussed this under business communication, both written and oral, but to summarize:

- You must give a good image of the organization by dress, appearance, communication skills.
- Do not become too familiar, but smile, be courteous and acknowledge customers/clients by surname if known.
- Respond to signals of non-verbal communication (facial expressions, body movements, sighs) which are often shown if someone is impatient or tired of waiting. A word of reassurance may ease the situation.
- Remember to use discretion when giving out information.

THINK! Is it confidential? Be tactful in difficult situations.

►ELECTRONIC COMMUNICATIONS

Many organizations today send written information from A to B using the telephone network. The chief advantage is that the written word can be transmitted as quickly as the spoken word on the telephone, because the text is converted into a series of electronic pulses or signals that can be transmitted over the telecommunications network. However, just as before you can make a telephone call you need a telephone, a telephone line and a telephone number, when you wish to transmit the written word you also need special equipment, a telephone line and compatible equipment to communicate with. Let us look more closely at how to transmit and receive copies of documents electronically.

Facsimile telegraphy (fax)

Facsimile (abbreviation: fax) means an exact copy and this is exactly what faxing a copy of a document does: it produces an exact copy for the recipient. A document is fed into the transmitting machine, this is converted into a series of electronic pulses and a copy of it is produced on the receiving fax machine, which can be sited anywhere in the world provided there is a telephone line and electricity.

> *Fax is therefore ideal for sending or receiving urgent information that needs to be seen. The information can be in picture or diagram form.*

Many manufacturers produce fax machines, eg Panasonic, Brother, Canon, Sharp, and prices vary depending on the features required. All fax machines are desktop (Figure 2.27) and some are portable, allowing you to plug them in to any telephone socket. Some of the features now available are:

- An integrated telephone.
- A liquid crystal display that informs you what is happening, ie 'dialling . . . . ', 'transmitting to . . . . ', 'failed to connect'.
- Automatic document feeder for faxing more than one copy.
- Paper cutter.
- Most fax machines take up to A4 paper, but some take up to size B4 for computer listing paper.
- Automatic redial facility.
- Automatic timer, so that the machine can be programmed to send a fax at a certain time, eg after office hours.
- Print a transmission report to confirm that the fax has been sent.
- Copier facility, so that the fax can be used to take a straight copy.

How to send a fax

Always refer to the manufacturer's handbook, but whichever fax machine you use the following will apply.

1   Check the document to be sent. Fax machines will only accept one sheet at a time, ie not a booklet, so take a photocopy first if necessary. Ensure that the document is not creased or torn as this may cause it to jam in the machine. If so take a photocopy first and use this. Ensure that the document to be transmitted is clear to read. If not, you may have to rewrite or retype. If the document is of poor quality then the transmitted copy will be even harder to read! Check the document to be sent is in blue or black print, other colours do not always fax well.

2   Check the recipient's fax number. Refer to the recipient's headed stationery, this often gives the fax number. Consult the fax directory: this is just like the telephone directory. Unfortunately this does not contain all fax numbers as fax users have to request that their number be entered. Telephone the organization and ask them for their fax number. Write the number down.

Figure 2.27 *British Telecom fax machine*

3   Prepare the fax header. Many organizations prepare a fax header or leader sheet (Figure 2.28), which is transmitted first to inform the receiving organization who the fax is from and who it is for. It also states the number of sheets to be transmitted.

4   Dial the fax number. (Note that some commonly used fax numbers may be stored in the fax memory and accessed through an abbreviated code.) The document should transmit automatically unless the line is engaged or there is some problem with the line, if so the machine will alert you to the fact that there is a problem on connecting. Redial.

51

FAX MESSAGE		
To	From	
Attention of	Originator	
No. of sheets	Fax No.	
Date	Time	Tel. No.
Message		

Figure 2.28 *A fax header sheet*

5 Await the transmission report. This will inform you of the date of transmission, the fax number you have transmitted to and the time taken. This is often filed, so that a record is kept of all fax transmissions and costs can be calculated. (However not all fax machines have this facility and you may have to request the machine to give you a report on all transmissions as required.)

How to receive a fax

1 Ensure your fax machine is switched on. If your fax machine is on a direct telephone line and switched on, then to receive a fax you really have little to do. Many organizations leave their machine switched on 24 hours a day, so that documents can be received even when the office is closed.

2   Check paper. All fax machines require special thermal paper. Do check there is sufficient paper in your machine.

3   Receiving a fax. Your machine will alert you to the fact that a fax is being transmitted. If you receive a header sheet then check that you have received the number of copies stated and fasten the header sheet to the transmitted documents. If there is any problem with the documents received, then contact the sender.

4   Record all transmissions. Some organizations log all documents received in a record book, together with details of the person/department they have been passed to.

5   Deliver documents/messages promptly. It is most important that the fax reaches its destination point as soon as possible and you should ensure that it is not left lying around. The main advantage of fax is its speed and if the message is not delivered quickly then it loses its impact.

Note:
It may be that your fax machine is plugged in to your telephone line and for a fax to be sent, the sender has to telephone you first and ask you to set the fax machine to receive. If this is the case, you must not replace the receiver until the fax has transmitted or you will 'cut the fax off', like a telephone call.

Telex

Telex precedes fax and is still the most widely used way of sending text messages overseas, because many organizations abroad have Telex machines but do not have fax. With the advancements in fax this situation may soon be reversed. With Telex you can only send **keyed in text** and not copies of documents, pictures or diagrams. For this reason Telex equipment used to consist of:

- A teleprinter (to print the message).
- A keyboard (to enter the message).
- A dialling unit (to dial the Telex number you wish to transmit to).

However, many modern Telex machines consist of:

- A VDU (so that messages can be altered and edited on screen).
- A disk drive (so messages may be prepared and stored on disk).
- A computer keyboard with dual purpose numeric key pad/dialling unit.
- A printer.

This means that the Telex machine (Figure 2.29) can also be used for basic word processing functions. Alternatively a desktop computer with a word processing package can have a Telex facility.

Figure 2.29 *A BT Cheetah Telex machine*

How to use Telex

You may hear people say that Telex is difficult to operate and requires specific training. This was true with the old type Telex equipment, where keying in had to be accurate and quick and Telex operators used special abbreviations to cut down the cost of sending messages. Some operators also used to prepare the message on punched tape, which encoded the message into a series of punched holes that could be transmitted much more quickly once prepared.

Now, if you can use a word processor, you will have no trouble using the modern Telex machines and even 'two fingered' keyboard operators can cope quite admirably with it. The message can be prepared on the VDU, altered as required, checked, stored on disk and then sent. Speed of input is therefore no longer important, but as you are charged on transmission time then the shorter the message the better, and abbreviations are quite acceptable.

Sending a Telex

1 Dial the Telex number. All Telex subscribers are allocated a Telex number and this can be found in the Telex Directory.

2 Wait for the Answerback code. This confirms that you are connected to the right machine. The code consists of three parts:

   a The Telex number.

   b An abbreviation of the company's name.

   c One or two letters to indicate the country.

3 Transmit the message either by direct keyboarding, or preferably from the computer memory. An example is given in Figure 2.30.

McGraw-Hill Book Company Europe

EDITORIAL DIVISION

Shoppenhangers Road, Maidenhead, Berkshire SL6 2QL
Telephone 0628 23432   Fax 0628 770224 Telex 848484

TELEX MESSAGE
Please advise immediately if transmission is incomplete or unclear

To Telex No	777891	Date	28 May 199*
Name	Susan Kennedy	From	Anthea Coombs
Location		Subject	Arrival of Mr Hill

Message

```
           MR HILL WILL ARRIVE JOHN KENNEDY AIRPORT NEW YORK FROM
           LONDON HEATHROW FLIGHT BA274 1300 HRS WED 4 JUNE.
           PLEASE COULD U ARRANGE HOTEL BOOKING FOR ONE NIGHT AND
           ARRANGE TRANSPORT FROM AIRPORT

           REGARDS




           ANTHEA
```

Figure 2.30 *Telex message*

Table 2.2 Comparison of fax, Telex and electronic mail

	Fax	Telex	Electronic mail
Confidentiality	Password commands are now being incorporated into some fax machines, but otherwise the transmitted document is visible for anyone to see. If the document is confidential then the sender would have to make verbal contact with the recipient and arrange when to send the fax.	Same problems with confidentiality as fax.	A password is needed to access the mailbox, therefore much more suitable for confidential messages. Caution must be taken when printing out messages.
Cost	Initial purchase or rental of equipment. Rental must be paid quarterly on the telephone line. Outgoing fax transmissions are then charged by British Telecom exactly the same as their telephone charges, according to time of day, distance and length of transmission. See chart Section 2. There is no charge for incoming transmissions, except that paper must be provided by the receiving fax. Fax paper is quite expensive.	Initial purchase or rental of equipment. Rental must be paid quarterly on Telex line. Calls are charged as follows: (as at 1.3.91) National calls 3.5p/60 seconds up to 35 miles. Over 35 miles 3.5p/20 seconds. International calls are charged in units of 6 seconds according to charge band.	Initial purchase or rental of equipment. Registration fee payable. Subscription payable usually monthly. Telecom Gold then charge for the number of characters transmitted: this varies depending on the time of day.

Advantages	Easy to use. Produces an exact copy, can transmit diagrams, tables, etc. Can communicate at any time: no problem with time differences.	Telex messages carry a sense of urgency, which means they are usually read and acted upon fast. Many subscribers worldwide. Clear and precise messaging. Multiple copies can be printed. Communication at any time: no problem with time differences.	Fast and confidential. No postal deadlines to meet. A copy of the message can be printed if required.
Disadvantages	The quality of copy is not as good as typescript. May be difficult to read if the copy is not clear. The fax copy will fade over a period of time.	Errors may be made by keyboard operator. Some training necessary. Will only transmit letters and numbers.	Subject to errors by keyboard operator. Limited number of subscribers. Will only transmit letters and numbers.

4 Exchange Answerback codes. This confirms that the message has been received.

Receiving a Telex

To receive a Telex follow the same procedure as receiving a fax.

Electronic mail

A simple definition of electronic mail is: *computers talking to each other through the telephone network*. A microcomputer is fitted with a modem that converts a digital signal from a computer into a signal which can then be transmitted along a standard telephone line. Organizations then subscribe to commercial organizations, for example British Telecom Gold, who have a control computer and when you register with them you are allocated a space on a disk in this computer, which is your **mailbox**. This is where messages from other users will be posted to you and stored. You then view your message from your own computer terminal using a password that you are allocated on registration. You can also print out your messages.

This is a very fast means of communication and your 'mailbox' is open 24 hours a day, so there are no postal deadlines. However, you can only communicate with other subscribers and this limits its use. It is also essential that the 'mailbox' is viewed frequently to ensure no correspondence is left unattended to.

Electronic mail is operated in a very similar way to Telex, only messages are keyed in and sent to the mailbox number rather than the Telex number.

Many organizations now use electronic mail internally. In other words computers within an organization are linked together so they can communicate with each other. This is then quicker than sending a memorandum, and cheaper and less time-consuming than making a telephone call.

Table 2.2 compares the advantages and disadvantages of fax, Telex and electronic mail for office use.

STORING AND RETRIEVING INFORMATION

► FILING

We are all involved with filing in our daily lives, although we may not realize it. From early days at school we probably kept different subject materials separate and at home we try to keep our clothes in specific places, **so we know where things are!** Think of going to the library and the way the books are classified on the shelves. This is so that they can be stored safely and retrieved when required. In business it is crucial that records and documents are filed away accurately and most people within an organization from the managing director to the junior clerk will be involved with filing. Filing is therefore an important job. Figure 3.1 illustrates why filing is so important in an organization.

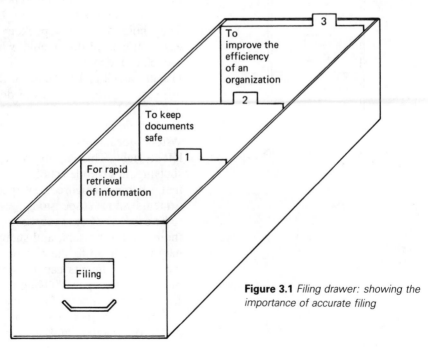

Figure 3.1 *Filing drawer: showing the importance of accurate filing*

Documents usually filed include: copies of letters, memoranda, orders, invoices, quotations, price lists, magazines, legal documents, personnel files, expense claim forms, company accounts.

▶ SETTING UP A FILING SYSTEM

Decide what equipment would be most appropriate to store the documents in.

> **THINK** about: Space available, cost, size and bulkiness of information to be stored, confidentiality of information, the number of people requiring access.

Equipment available

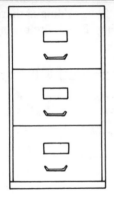

Figure 3.2 Vertical filing cabinets

Vertical filing cabinets. These are available in two, three or four drawer sizes, and in different designs and colours (see Figure 3.2). They hold suspension pockets for easy retrieval of documents, which are placed one behind the other. Usually metal and lockable so they are very secure. All types of documents can be stored.

Lateral filing cabinets. With this system documents are filed from left to right. This may be on open shelving, in a wooden cupboard or a metal cabinet (Figure 3.3) Special fitments allow suspension pockets to be used. They are space saving as there are no drawers, and shelving may be built up to the ceiling. All types of documents can be stored but obviously open shelving is not suitable for confidential documents.

Horizontal cabinets. These may be metal or wooden and in various

60

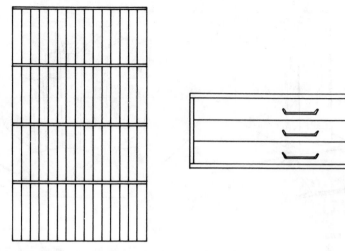

Figure 3.3 *Lateral filing cabinets*   **Figure 3.4** *Horizontal cabinets*

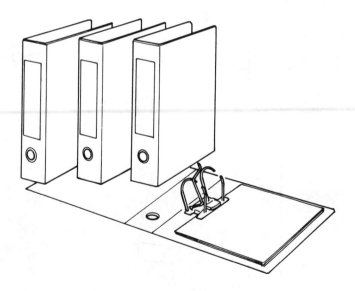

Figure 3.5 *Lever arch files*

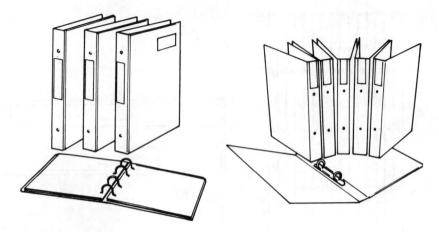

Figure 3.6 *A4 ring binders*

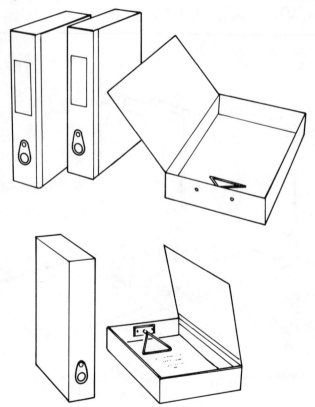

Figure 3.7 *Box files*

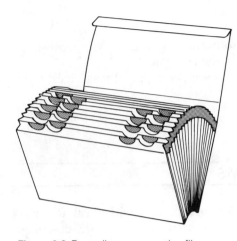

Figure 3.8 *Expanding or concertina files*

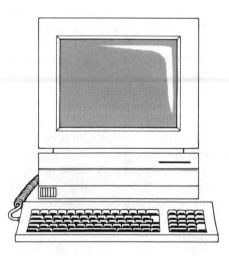

Figure 3.9 *Computerized filing system*

sizes and colours. The drawers are very shallow and wide (Figure 3.4) and therefore suitable for large documents, such as architect's plans. The documents are laid flat and filed one on top of the other.

Lever arch files, ring binders, box files. These files (Figures 3.5, 3.6 and 3.7) are commonly used at home and in the office and may be used in conjunction with other filing equipment. They are cheap and easy to label. Groups of papers such as invoices can be kept together in this way. If used by themselves the security aspect must be considered: fire, theft and confidentiality. They can get bulky and take up a lot of space: remember **safety** and do not store files where they will create a hazard.

Expanding or concertina files. As the name implies these files expand to give a series of pockets (Figure 3.8). They are usually made of card. They are useful for filing small numbers of lightweight documents, ie copies of letters, and are cheap and easy to carry around. The security aspect must be considered: fire, theft and confidentiality.

Computerized filing system. A database may be created to contain records, eg personnel records and customer details (see Figure 3.9). There are several advantages:

- Space-saving and time-saving.
- Information may be quickly retrieved from disk and accessed from desktop computers.
- Passwords allow information to be kept confidential.

Disadvantages include:

- Equipment, ie the computer and software may be initially expensive.
- Personnel need to be trained to use the equipment.
- Not all information can be stored this way, eg copies of magazines, legal documents.

▶ CLASSIFICATION SYSTEMS

Decide the best way to store the documents, ie classify them for easy retrieval. The classification systems most commonly used are described below.

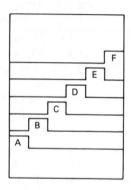

Figure 3.10 *Alphabetical system*

				0108
			0107	
		0106		
	0105			
0104		.		
0103				
0102				
0101				
0100				

Figure 3.11 *Numerical system*

Alphabetical General alphabetical filing (Figure 3.10) is the placing of documents in strict alphabetical order of name, whether surname, company name, magazine title. An example is names in a telephone directory.

Numerical Each file, document, magazine is allocated a number and then the files are placed in the filing system in numerical order (Figure 3.11). This is particularly useful for large filing systems, as it is easier to expand the system and file with greater accuracy. The file number may also be used as a reference on all correspondence. However, it is essential that any numerical filing system has an alphabetical index. Hospital records and copies of orders and invoices are usually filed in this way.

Geographical With this method files are arranged in alphabetical

Derby
Crewe
Congleton
Carlisle
Bootle
Birkenhead

Figure 3.12 *Geographical system*

Typewriters
Tables (writing)
Tables (coffee)
Desks
Chairs (typing)
Chairs (reception)
Chairs (executive)
Cabinets

Figure 3.13 *Alphabetical by subject system*

8.7.88
7.10.88
4.11.88
5.6.89
17.10.89
20.10.89
23.9.90
25.9.90

Figure 3.14 *Chronological (date order) system*

order, according to location, ie the town (as in Figure 3.12), county, country. A travel agent may file holiday brochures in this way. Sales departments may also find it useful to file correspondence relating to sales representatives and their territories in geographical order.

Subject This is a method of arranging files in alphabetical order according to subject or topic (Figure 3.13). Purchasing departments may use this way to file advertisement literature received on, for example, office equipment.

Chronological This is filing in date order (Figure 3.14). It is often used in conjunction with other classification systems, ie within a file the papers are placed in date order **with the most recent on top**. Magazines and trade journals and documents relating to buying and selling may be filed in this way.

Rules for filing alphabetically

1 File according to **surname** and then in order of the first names or initials:

Kennedy
Kennedy A
Kennedy Andrew
Kennedy P
Kennedy P J

2 If a company has initials only, file according to the initials in alphabetical sequence:

Brown & Co. Ltd
BT Industries plc
BTS Industries Co. Ltd

3 One letter comes before 'more than one letter':

F & B Industries
FAB Industries

4 Usually names beginning with prefixes like Mac, Mack or Mc are all treated as if they are spelt Mac and placed in front of the M file.

5 Usually names containing the word Saint or St, eg St James' church are all filed as if spelt Saint.

6 A and The in front of a name are ignored in filing and placed at the back of the title:

Kennedy Publishing Co. Ltd, The

7 Titles of people are also placed behind the surname and ignored for filing purposes:

Kennedy, Sir James

8 Numbers are filed as if they were words. For example: 2000 Dance Studio would become Two Thousand Dance Studio (file under T).

9 Treat **hyphenated names** and names that have a **prefix** as if they are complete words:

Parker-Brown would become Parkerbrown (file under P)
O'Connell would become Oconnell (file under O).

▶ TIPS ON MAINTAINING A FILING SYSTEM

- File daily.
- Look for release symbol (this indicates that a file has been dealt with and may be filed: see Glossary).
- Look for the filing point: see Glossary.
- When filing alphabetically follow the rules given.
- Establish a booking-out system to use when files are borrowed from your system. This may involve inserting an 'out card' showing the file name, number, the name of the borrower, their department or position and the date. See example in Glossary.
- Follow up files that have been borrowed from your system and ask the borrower to return them after a reasonable period of time.
- Find out your organization's file retention policy. How long must you keep files and documents for? This will enable you to remove out-of-date documents and files and keep your filing system more efficient. Some companies will transfer files that are not in current use to a separate storage area.
- Confidentiality: check on who is allowed access to files and how you are to dispose of 'dead' files. See Glossary.

> **REMEMBER!** *Be accurate: if you are not sure ask. A document or file misplaced could lose business and waste a lot of time.*

Glossary of filing terms

Centralized filing This is where:

- All filing takes place in one department.
- All information is therefore kept in one place and staff know exactly where to find it.
- A standardized system of classification may be employed and staff are usually trained in how to use it.
- Staff may be employed to work purely in this department and are therefore highly motivated to maintain an efficient filing system.
- Specialized staff make cross-referencing and keeping records of file movements easier.

Cross-referencing Sometimes letters and documents could be filed under more than one heading or name, ie A & A Software Ltd may be filed alphabetically under 'A' or 'Software'. A cross-reference sheet should be inserted where the file is not stored, stating where it is. This saves time looking for files and leads to an efficient system.

Dead files   A term used for files that are out of date and no longer required in the current filing system. These files may be transferred to another storage area or destroyed. Alternatively, some organizations now choose to have files microfilmed and in this way the documents can be retained, but stored in a much smaller area.

Filing point   This is the item in the document that tells you how to classify it. In other words if you are filing alphabetically under name, the filing point on a letter will be the name of the person or organization sending it. If you are filing numerically, check to see if they have typed your ref. on the letter; the reference will be the number it is filed under and therefore the filing point. Pre-sort documents according to their filing point before taking them to the filing system.

Indexing   An indexing system is used to keep records that will help the user to find further information in a filing system. For example, if files are classified numerically and you do not know the file number you would have difficulty locating them unless you kept an alphabetical index of names. This index may be kept in various ways:

- Very simply on record cards in an index box (Figure 3.15).

Figure 3.15 *Index box*

- On a visible edge card index system (Figure 3.16).
- On a strip index.
- On a rotary card index (Figure 3.17).
- On a computerized database.

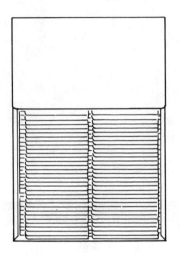

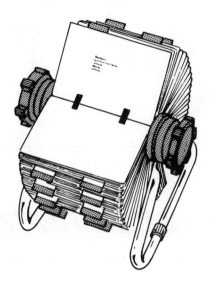

Figure 3.16 *Visible edge card index system*   **Figure 3.17** *Rotary card index*

Miscellaneous file   This is used when there are too few related documents to create an individual file. Papers are placed in alphabetical order in a miscellaneous file and when there are four to five related documents these can be transferred to their own file. A convenient method of storing these miscellaneous papers is in an expanding or concertina wallet file.

Out card   This card shows who has borrowed a file, and is inserted where the file should be (see Figure 3.18).

Pending file   Used to store letters or documents relating to work in progress or documents to be dealt with. Very often this file takes the form of a tray on the boss's desk. In other words these documents have not been released for filing.

Release symbol   This indicates that a document has been dealt with and may be filed. These symbols vary from organization to organization and may be a line through the paper, F for file, the initials of the receiver or the word 'file' stamped on the document.

File name .... No.			
Date	**Borrowed by**	**Department**	**Returned on**

Figure 3.18 *Out card*

Additional notes on filing

Add below any notes that you would like to make on filing.

MAIL HANDLING

Sending information by post is much slower than using the telephone or communicating electronically and in general takes at least one or two days to arrive. However, it is still the most widely used method of sending written information from A to B and as it is the same price to send a letter anywhere in the UK it can also work out the cheapest. Every organization receives and sends mail and the handling of mail will vary depending upon the size and type of organization.

1   Some organizations will have a specific **mail room** where all incoming and outgoing mail is dealt with.

2   In other organizations, the mail may be delivered to the receptionist who will sort it, ready for individuals to collect.

3   The person who is first in the office opens and distributes the mail.

4   In some offices the manager prefers to open and distribute all mail. In other cases this task may be delegated to the office junior.

5   Individuals may be responsible for posting their own letters, or one person may be allocated this responsibility: the secretary, the office junior or a specific mail clerk.

▶ THE MAIL ROOM

Most organizations large enough to be divided in to departments have a mail room where letters and parcels are delivered by The Post Office and where all outgoing mail is stamped or franked, before being taken to the local post office. Staff working in a mail room must be efficient so that mail is dealt with promptly, both incoming and outgoing. In a large firm, mail room staff may take it in turns to come in before other office staff, in order to make sure that all the mail has been taken round to the departments by the time the office staff are ready to start. They will also collect outgoing mail from departments at fixed times each day.

Mail room equipment

Even the smallest mail room will probably include the following equipment and fittings, for these are essential for the smooth and efficient processing of incoming and outgoing mail.

1 A large table/tables for sorting the mail.

2 Trays or 'pigeon-holes' to sort the mail into departments or for individual members of staff. 'Pigeon-holes' is the name commonly given to the style of shelving that the mail is placed in, as illustrated in Figure 4.1.

Sales		Personnel		Purchasing	
Accounts		Catering		Office manager	
Laboratory		Managing director		Company secretary	

Figure 4.1 *Pigeon-holes*

3 Trolley for delivering and collecting mail from departments.

4 A date stamp, which may also include the time.

5 A paper knife to open the envelopes or an electric letter opener, which shears a very fine shaving from the edge of each envelope.

> **IMPORTANT** *When using an electric letter opener, tap the envelope on the table first to ensure the contents fall away from the top edge and thus avoid cutting the letter into pieces.*

6 Scales: essential for weighing letters and small parcels, in order to calculate the postage rate. These may be traditional balance scales (Figure 4.2) or electronic (Figure 4.3). The advantage with electronic scales is that

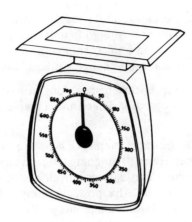

Figure 4.2 *Balance scales*

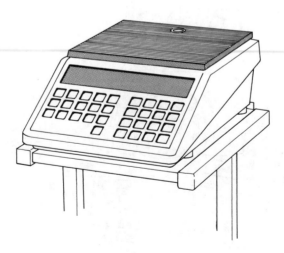

Figure 4.3 *Electronic scales*

they will work out the postage rate for you, provided you depress the correct keys to say whether it is to go first or second class, airmail, parcel rate, etc. The scales contain a microchip with the up-to-date postal rates and every time the postal rates change you are issued with a new one.

7 A stapler for fastening enclosures. A long-arm stapler would also be useful for large or awkward packages and a staple extractor to save the finger nails.

8 A franking machine (postage meter). These are very common in most organizations that have over 10 outgoing letters a day. The machine prints a form of postage stamp and date on envelopes or on strips of gummed paper and saves having to affix postage stamps. It is therefore much quicker and gives mail a business-like image. The machine will also keep an accurate record of the amount of postage purchased and spent. Standard features to be found on most franking machines are described below and shown in Figure 4.4.

a Ascending and descending register to show the postage as it is used and the credit balance remaining.

b Can feed any size of envelope through but for packages and parcels frank adhesive labels.

c An advertising slogan or return address can be printed on the envelope.

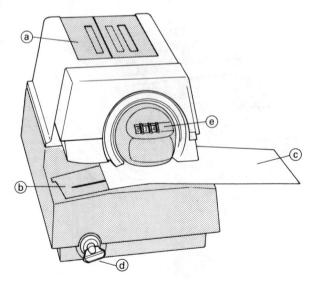

Figure 4.4 *Franking machine*

d A key ensures that the machine can be locked when not in use.

e The amount of postage can be selected very easily.

Postage still has to be purchased from The Post Office or the supplier in units. Some machines have to be taken to the local post office where the clerk will update the meter and lock the number of units purchased in to the machine since the post office will hold the only keys. Some machines can now be updated by a computer link with the supplier and this saves having to take the machine to a post office. The meter records the number of units of postage the machine has in credit and every time the machine is used this figure will reduce by the number of units used, this is called the **descending register**. There is also a second meter, called the **ascending register**, which keeps a record of the amount of postage as it is used, so, as the name implies, this will go up as the credit meter goes down.

Tips on using the franking machine

- Check the meter regularly to ensure that you have sufficient credit. Ask staff to let you know in advance if they are going to have a 'big mail shot' so that you do not run out of credit.
- Change the date each day as a matter of routine.
- Check the postage value: it is easy to waste postage by forgetting that the value is set for first class, when you require second class.
- Ensure that there is sufficient ink in the machine to give a good impression: with most modern franking machines this is very clean and simple to do. Your equipment manual will tell you how to do this.
- Sort the franked mail into first and second class. The post office will usually give you red bags into which all first class post is to be placed and green bags into which all second class post is to be placed.
- Take the mail to the post office or arrange for it to be collected. You must not place franked mail in the post box. This also gives you the opportunity to take any recorded or registered mail, as these items cannot be franked.

> Some organizations will have more sophisticated franking machines that will carry out some or all of the following features:
> - fold the letters
> - insert the letters into the envelopes
> - seal the envelopes
> - weigh the mail
> - frank with appropriate value.

9 Additional mail room equipment may include the following.

a Addressing machines for printing names and addresses on envelopes, labels and cards.

b Folding machines for folding papers ready to insert into envelopes.

c Envelope sealing machines to moisten and seal envelopes.

d Inserting and sealing machines, which will insert documents into envelopes, seal, stack and count.

e A large waste paper bin.

The following checklist will help you ensure that you have sufficient materials in your stationery cupboard to cope with all aspects of mail handling.

A variety of envelopes (manilla or white), eg

.... C6 $4\frac{1}{2} \times 6\frac{3}{8}''$ plain

.... DL $4\frac{1}{4} \times 8\frac{5}{8}''$ plain

.... DL $4\frac{1}{4} \times 8\frac{5}{8}''$ window

.... C4 $12\frac{3}{4} \times 9''$ plain

.... POCKET $9'' \times 4''$ plain

.... A variety of padded bags or air bubble bags in different sizes

.... Packing list envelopes (Figure 4.5)

.... Franking labels $5\frac{1}{2} \times 1\frac{1}{2}''$

.... Address labels

.... Brown paper and packing material

.... Marker pen

.... Adhesive tape and brown sealing tape for parcels

.... String

.... Rubber bands

.... Scissors

.... Staples

.... Paper clips

.... An envelope moistener (Figure 4.6)

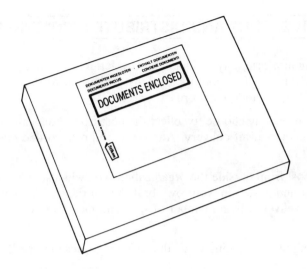

Figure 4.5 *Packing list envelope*

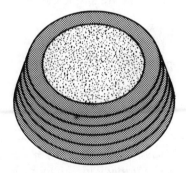

Figure 4.6 *An envelope moistener*

Handling the mail is a very important job and it is necessary to have rules and procedures so that the job is carried out efficiently. The following information may be of help to you, but do check the procedure in your own organization.

▶ RECEIVE, SORT AND DISTRIBUTE INCOMING MAIL

Mail arriving at a firm may include invoices, letters (including some marked private and confidential), job applications, orders, advertisement material, money, eg cheques and postal orders, parcels.

The organization may choose to collect the post from the local postal sorting office, rather than await delivery. Any registered or recorded mail will have to be signed for.

As well as post from outside the organization, you will also have to deal with internal post and post from your own branches or depots. To avoid postage, this is often delivered by a member of staff and may therefore arrive at any time.

When dealing with incoming mail, the following rules may be helpful.

1 Do not open any correspondence marked 'Private', 'Confidential', 'Personal'. Deliver it unopened to the person it is addressed to.

2 Look out for any unusual packages (poorly wrapped, poorly addressed, unusual post mark) and if you are suspicious ask your supervisor or boss for their advice.

3 Open the mail if this is your organization's policy. If not proceed to step 4.

   a Open each envelope carefully with a paper knife or electric letter opener.

   b Take out the contents and attach any enclosures with a stapler.

> **THINK!** Use your common sense: if a stapler will damage the contents, then secure firmly with a paper clip or bulldog clip.

   c Make sure the envelope is empty.

   d Date stamp each document, but not cheques.

   e Where a cheque or money is enclosed, details should be entered in a special book, called a remittance book (see Figure 4.7).

   f If a letter mentions an enclosure, but this has not been sent then make a note of this in pencil at the foot of the letter. Initial your comment and inform your supervisor.

REMITTANCE BOOK

Date	Sender	Method of payment	Amount	Signature
3/5/9	Oxy Components Ltd	Cheque	£256.34	G. Smith
3/5/9	Rose Foods Ltd	Cheque	£106.92	G. Smith
3/5/9	Aero Products (UK) Ltd	BACS-Credit transfer	£505.50	G. Smith

Figure 4.7 *A page from a remittance book*

Note:
It is important to check the procedure for handling remittances with your organization. In some organizations the money will go with the opened letter to the addressee and is eventually passed on to the accounts department. In other organizations, the person handling the incoming mail will be responsible for passing all remittances received to the accounts department. In this case the amount received and the initials of the person opening the letter should be written in pencil at the foot of the letter and any queries regarding the remittance should be referred to the accounts department. In a small organization, it may be that if you open the mail, you are also responsible for dealing with any queries over remittances, ie contacting the sender yourself, and it may also be your responsibility to deposit the money at the bank.

4 Sort the correspondence into departments. An organization chart will be of great help here, until you are familiar with the organization (see Section 1). Look for the following to help you decide where to send it:

a An attention line or salutation.

b A subject heading.

c 'Your ref.': this will give an indication of who the letter is replying to.

d The content of the correspondence: who would be the best person to deal with it? It may be that the correspondence needs to be seen by more than one person, for example, advertisement literature, change in customer details, 'Thank you' letters. In this case you can do one of the following:

  i Photocopy it and send each person/department a copy.
  ii Use a **circulation slip**. List the people/departments who you think should see the correspondence and attach the slip (Figure 4.8) to the correspondence. Take it to the first person on the slip and then they are responsible for passing it on to the next person on the list. They tick or initial that they have seen it before they pass it on. This obviously takes more time than a photocopy, but may be more convenient if the item is a brochure or multiple page document.

CIRCULATION SLIP		
Item: *BE SAFE* Magazine	Received on: 22.3.9*	
Please read and pass on in the order shown below		
Name	Department	Initials
P. Smith	Personnel	
R. Hunt	Health and safety	
T. Parker	Security	
C. Ryan	Reception	

Figure 4.8 *Circulation slip*

Take your time over sorting the mail: any carelessness could lead to a great deal of time being wasted by other members of staff.

5 Fasten the sorted correspondence together with elastic bands, or place in appropriate trays. Remember to include the unopened Private, Confidential or Personal letters and arrange for the mail to be delivered or collected as quickly as possible.

▶ DESPATCH OUTGOING/INTERNAL MAIL

If you are responsible for handling outgoing mail, then your busiest time is likely to be late afternoon, when everyone rushes to catch that evening's post. To avoid a sudden rush of mail, a system of regular collection from every person/department should be organized.

In some organizations, letters are sent to the mail room already folded and inserted in envelopes with a pencilled '1' or '2' in the top right-hand corner to show whether the letter has to go by first or second class post. In other organizations letters and other documents are sent to the mail room accompanied by correctly typed envelopes and the mail room clerk's job is to fold and insert the letters in to the envelopes. While doing this the rules given in Figure 4.9 overleaf should be observed.

Dealing with urgent mail

If you are dealing with urgent mail then consider the following services.

Courier service There are numerous private companies who offer a door-to-door delivery service on letters and packages of all sizes. A variety of services are usually offered and charged accordingly, same day, next day, 2–3 day delivery. Some courier services are local, others national and others international. Many of the couriers use motorbikes for the delivery of small packages. Check with your local directories and newspapers to find details of courier services.

Royal Mail services *Datapost* for the delivery of urgent letters and parcels in the UK and world-wide. Delivery is guaranteed next day in the UK (by 10 am to all main areas). *Special Delivery* is another service offered for first class letters. For an extra fee delivery is guaranteed on the first working day after you post the letter, provided you meet the postal deadline. If it is not delivered next day the Post Office will refund your fee. *Swiftair* is a priority

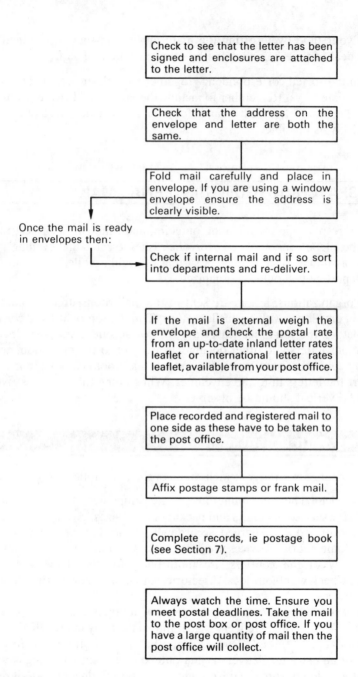

Check to see that the letter has been signed and enclosures are attached to the letter.

Check that the address on the envelope and letter are both the same.

Fold mail carefully and place in envelope. If you are using a window envelope ensure the address is clearly visible.

Once the mail is ready in envelopes then:

Check if internal mail and if so sort into departments and re-deliver.

If the mail is external weigh the envelope and check the postal rate from an up-to-date inland letter rates leaflet or international letter rates leaflet, available from your post office.

Place recorded and registered mail to one side as these have to be taken to the post office.

Affix postage stamps or frank mail.

Complete records, ie postage book (see Section 7).

Always watch the time. Ensure you meet postal deadlines. Take the mail to the post box or post office. If you have a large quantity of mail then the post office will collect.

Figure 4.9 *Mail room rules*

airmail letter service; *Swiftair* items are dealt with as quickly as possible, but a particular delivery time cannot be guaranteed.

Red Star   A service offered by British Rail for sending parcels station to station. The parcel must be marked with the name of recipient (not address) and the destination station. The sender's name and address should also be shown. The sender selects the train time to be used from the British Rail Red Star Station to Station timetable and takes the parcel to the Red Star Parcel Point at the station, at least 30 minutes before the scheduled train departure time. The sender must then inform the recipient when and where to collect the parcel. The recipient must produce evidence of identity and authority to collect. Red Star will also collect and deliver. Prices are based on weight and full details are available from British Rail.

Wrapping a parcel

Wrapping a birthday present is one thing, but wrapping an item that is to be handled with thousands of others and has to travel by road or train and perhaps abroad is another. The following steps are recommended:

1   Use a strong box, unless the item is soft and unbreakable. Boxes can be purchased from main post offices.

2   If a box is not used, wrap the item in corrugated paper and strong brown paper.

3   Pack the box with soft material, such as newspaper, tissues, corrugated paper, polystyrene chips, so that the contents are protected and cannot move around inside the box.

4   For small items a padded bag may be used.

5   Seal the box/package firmly along all flaps and edges with strong self-adhesive tape of a good width.

6   If a box is not used it is advised that in addition to self-adhesive tape string is tied firmly around the package.

7   Address the parcel clearly with the name of the post town in capitals. Use the postcode.

8   Include your own address on the outside, usually the reverse, of packaging, marked **sender**.

9   It is recommended that your address and the recipient's address should be attached to the article **inside** the parcel. This is particularly important if the parcel is to be sent abroad.

Sending letters abroad via the post office

Use airmail labels if sending items abroad or write **Par Avion/By Airmail** in the top left-hand corner. Books and newspapers should not be sealed, so that they are easy to open for examination. Choose the service you require:

- Airmail: delivery normally two to four days for Europe, two to seven days for cities outside Europe.
- Swiftair: express delivery service, no guaranteed delivery time.
- Surface mail: cheaper, but delivery within 2 weeks to Europe and up to 12 weeks outside Europe.

► POST OFFICE SERVICES

The Post Office guide will give you details of all Post Office services. Below is a summary of some of the frequently used ones.

First class post   Charged according to the weight of the letter. Check with inland letter rates leaflet. The Post Office aim to deliver first class letters the first working day after collection.

Second class post   This service is again according to the weight of the letter, but is a lot cheaper. Check with inland letter rates leaflet. However, it takes longer and The Post Office aim to deliver second class letters the third working day after collection.

Certificate of posting   This is a way of proving that an important letter has been posted, but does not prove that it has been delivered. The service is **free** and the letter must be handed in at a post office counter for the counter clerk to issue you with an authorized receipt.

Recorded delivery   This service provides proof of posting and delivery. A fee is paid and the post office counter clerk issues you with a receipt and also authorizes the postman to collect a signature from the recipient. It is useful when sending documents and papers of little or no direct monetary value, but which could cause a great deal of inconvenience if lost, eg passport, examination papers, birth certificate.

Registered mail   This provides proof of posting and delivery, plus compensation if the item is lost in the post. A fee is paid according to the amount of compensation required. Special envelopes may be used and are available at the post office. It is particularly useful when sending money, jewellery or other valuable items.

Advice of delivery   If you wish to be informed that items you have sent by registered or recorded mail have been delivered, then you must complete an advice of delivery form available at post offices and pay an additional fee at the time of posting.

Freepost An organization wishing to obtain a reply from a customer/client without putting that customer to the expense of paying postage may include in his address the word **Freepost**. The reply bearing this word can then be posted in the ordinary way, but without a stamp. The organization receiving the letter pays the postage to The Post Office. A licence is needed before an organization can use the Freepost service.

Business reply service Again this is for organizations who wish to obtain replies from customers/clients without putting them to the expense of postage. Specially printed postcards, envelopes or labels are required, bearing the organization's licence number, address and marked first or second class. The envelope is posted in the normal way and postage is paid by the organization receiving the mail.

Poste restante A person who travels around the country may arrange for mail to be sent to a named post office from which it can be collected. This service is not charged for, provided it is not used with the same post office for longer than three months. Items must be collected within two weeks otherwise they are returned to the sender. Type the words **poste restante** on the envelope and type your own address on the back.

Private boxes Many organizations choose to have a private box and you will often see this as part of company addresses, eg 'reply to PO Box 147'. This can serve two purposes: 1 Mail may be collected from the box at any time of the day and you do not have to wait for deliveries. 2 The address of the company stays anonymous. These boxes are rented from The Post Office.

IMPORTANT Do check with your post office: they have numerous free leaflets that give information about all their services.

STOCK HANDLING

▶ OFFICE EQUIPMENT AND MATERIALS

Imagine working in an office and not having a piece of paper to type a letter on, or an envelope to post the letter in. To run out of office materials would bring production in an office to a stop, just as a factory would halt production if the parts they required were not available. It is therefore very important that someone in an organization is responsible for keeping a stock of office materials required, issuing these to staff as requested, and restocking so that the organization does not run out. This is what we mean by **stock control**: ensuring that a sufficient quantity is always available when needed, but ensuring that not too many goods are purchased that would tie up the organization's money and storage space in unnecessary stock.

Depending on the size of the organization you work for you may be:

1 Responsible for keeping all items of stationery within a department.

2 Responsible for keeping all items of stationery for the whole organization.

This will involve the processes and arrangements shown in Figure 5.1.

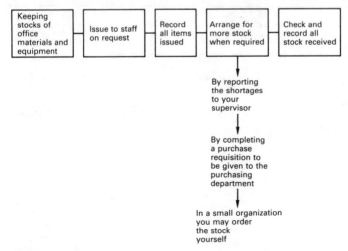

Figure 5.1 *Stock handling*

86

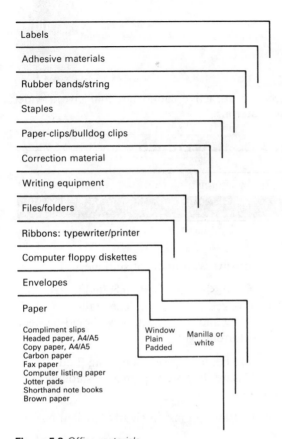

Figure 5.2 *Office materials*

Firstly, let us consider the items of office materials and equipment we are likely to keep as stock. The items shown in Figure 5.2 are frequently used, but the list is by no means exhaustive. In other words depending on the work of the organization more items may be required. You will be guided by your supervisor.

Office materials are often referred to as office consumables, because these are items that, generally, once used, cannot be used again, eg a piece of paper can only be used once or paper-clips/rubber bands are not returned. Most of the selection shown in Figure 5.2 are office consumables.

On the other hand, office equipment can be used time and time again and these items will be issued less frequently. Usually only small items of office equipment will be kept in stock, for example:

- Staplers.
- Scissors.

- Index card boxes.
- Diskette boxes.
- Letter trays.
- Paper punch.

Office equipment suppliers produce attractive catalogues that give a wide choice of office equipment and materials.

► HANDLING STOCK

Storing the stock

1 Think of safety and security.

   a Do not block corridors or doorways with items of stationery.

   b Keep stock in locked cabinets with shelves clearly labelled to keep the items tidy, or preferably in a locked store room. The stationery clerk should be responsible for the key and a duplicate key should be kept with a senior member of staff for emergencies.

   c Do not store paper/inflammable liquids (spirit duplicating fluid, cleaning materials) near a heater. Ensure they are kept in a no-smoking area and clearly marked **inflammable**.

   d Keep sharp items, eg scissors, drawing pins, in clearly labelled boxes.

2 Think of access.

   a Ensure that frequently used items are easy to get to.

   b Label where items of stationery are to be stored and keep them tidily in their proper places.

   c Do not place heavy items on high shelves.

   d Ensure that if you do have to store stock on high shelves, you have a suitable step-ladder with which to reach them.

Issuing stock

Stock requisition note

In most organizations stock will only be issued against a requisition note for stock. This note is very useful as it serves the dual purpose of providing an accurate record of the materials required and a check can be kept on who is ordering stock and the frequency to try to avoid pilfering and wastage. As an additional security feature it may be that the requisition note has to be authorized by a senior member of staff.

A stock requisition note can be designed and printed internally and may be either very brief or detailed like the examples shown in Figures 5.3 and 5.4.

Shepperton Industries PLC
Stationery requisition form
Name .... Date ....
Dept .... Reqd by ....
Please supply the following:

Qty	Description

Signature ....
Authorized by ....

Figure 5.3 *Simple stationery requisition form*

If the brief type shown in Figure 5.3 is used then it is important to circulate staff with detailed lists of stock items that are available, so that the note can be completed correctly.

The detailed requisition form gives a list of items carried in stock (Figure 5.4). These are often printed on duplicate paper so that a copy can be kept by the Stock Clerk and a copy returned with the completed order.

Shepperton Industries PLC

Stationery requisition

Please supply the following items

Name ....

Dept .... Required by ....

Paper	Qty
A4 Headed paper (ream).......................	....
A5 Headed paper (1/2 ream)...................	....
A4 White copy paper (ream)...................	....
A5 White copy paper (1/2 ream)...............	....
Shorthand note books.........................	....
Telephone message pads.......................	....
A4 Carbon paper (pkt 20 sheets)..............	....
A4 Computer listing paper (1000 sheets)......	....

Envelopes
Manilla pocket DL 8 5/8 x 4 1/4" (pkt 100)........... ....
White wallet DL (pkt 100)......................... ....
Manilla pocket C4 123/4 x 9" (pkt 25)................ ....

Correction fluid..................................... ....
Correction paper..................................... ....
Staples (box).. ....
Paper-clips (box).................................... ....
Rubber bands (pkt)................................... ....
Clear adhesive tape 1" x 72 yds...................... ....
Vinyl adhesive tape 2" x 72 yds...................... ....
Black ball pen....................................... ....
Black marker pen..................................... ....

Additional items

....

....

Authorized by : .... Date ....

Figure 5.4 *Detailed stationery requisition form*

Dealing with unavailable items

There may be two reasons why a requested item is unavailable.

1 It is not normally required and therefore not kept as a stock item.

2 You are out of stock because your supplier has not delivered on time but the item is required urgently.

> *Firstly inform your supervisor if you have one. It may be possible to contact the supplier who will arrange for special delivery. If this is not possible or for 'one-off' items seek permission to draw the money from petty cash and purchase the item required.*

Recording stock issued

It is extremely important to have a record, so that instead of physically counting the stock items, you know exactly at any one time how much stock you have. It will also ensure that you do not re-order too much stock since this not only costs the organization money but can cause storage problems.

The stock record card

Keep a stock record card, like the one shown in Figure 5.5, for each stock item. The card should show the minimum amount below which the stock should not fall and the maximum amount likely to be required. These figures will be decided by your supervisor or through experience. However, for frequently used items, it is better to calculate a **re-order level** that ensures you allow time for the processing of the order and delivery, before you reach the minimum level. To calculate the re-order level, find the average daily usage, multiply this by the normal delivery time and add on the minimum stock level.

Example: *A4 copier paper.*
The organization uses approximately two reams a day. Delivery is three days. Minimum stock is 10 reams. The re-order level would be: $2 \times 3 + 10 = 16$.

> *Note*:
> These stock cards may be kept manually in a card index system or on a database on computer. Alternatively a stock control package or integrated software accounts package can be used, but these are generally more appropriate when the goods are stocked for resale or you are issuing a lot of stock items, for example, in a production department.

SHEPPERTON INDUSTRIES PLC

STATIONERY STOCK CARD

Item *A4 White copier paper* .... Max. stock *50 reams*

Ref. no. *CopA4W* .... Min. stock *10 reams*

Supplier *Penard's Office Supplies* .... Re-order level *16*

Brasenose Street

Bootle

Receipts		Issues			Balance	Order No. and date
Date	Qty recvd	Date	Qty	To		
8/3	50				50	
		9/3	1	*Accounts*	49	
		9/3	1	*Sales*	48	
		10/3	2	*Typing pool*	46	

Figure 5.5 *Stock card*

Requesting more stock

The methods for requesting more stock will depend on the organization you work for. You may

1 Inform your supervisor what stock is required.

2 Complete a purchase requisition for the purchasing department (see

Figure 5.6). This will give details of the item and quantity, together with the date when delivery is required. If known, it will also state the usual supplier. From this information the purchasing department will produce an order (see Section 6).

SHEPPERTON INDUSTRIES PLC

SHEPPERTON HOUSE
APPELTON INDUSTRIAL ESTATE   WA3 2BP

PURCHASE REQUISITION

From: Christine Whaley .....

Requisition no: 125 ....

Dept: Administration .....

Date: .23.March.199* ....

[Supplier   ]
Penard's Office Supplies
Brasenose Street
Bootle

[   ]

Please order the following:

Qty	Description	Comments
34 reams	A4 White copier paper	3 day delivery service

Signature .C.Whaley..........

Authorized by ....

Position ....

Figure 5.6 *Purchase requisition*

93

3 Order the goods yourself, in which case see Section 6. Ordering goods and services.

Receiving and checking new stock

All organizations have their own procedure for receiving new stock but the following will generally apply.

Goods received note

If you placed the order yourself, check the goods carefully when they are delivered against the original order form. The goods should be as ordered and in good condition. If so then it is usual to enter the details on a **goods received note** and pass a copy of this to the accounts department who will check it against the purchase invoice (see Section 6). If there are any errors in the delivery then contact the supplier. Under the Sale of Goods Act 1979, if you receive faulty goods or the goods are not as ordered the supplier must exchange them or refund your money.

If the goods were ordered through the purchasing department, check them carefully against your purchase requisition form and check their condition. Record the goods received on a goods received note and state any shortages or damage. Pass the completed goods received note to the purchasing department who will check it against the original order and follow up any discrepancies. Once the purchasing department are satisfied they will pass it to the accounts department.

> **IMPORTANT** *It is vital that you enter the stock received on your stock record cards as soon as possible.*

Stock check

Even though records are kept of stock, at least once a year an inventory should be carried out. This means that a list must be drawn up of all items of stock and the items must be counted. The figures will then be compared with the stock record cards. The physical check is obviously going to be the accurate record and any discrepancies are likely to be due to:

- Goods having been issued without a requisition note.
- Information incorrectly entered on record cards.
- Information not entered on record cards.
- Theft.

Tips on handling stock

- Remember that a ream of paper is 500 sheets.
- Boxes of paper containing five or ten reams of paper can be very heavy, so lift by bending your knees.
- Rotate the stock. Issue old stock before new.
- If you are handling stock other than stationery and office equipment then the procedure will still be the same as that described in this section.

ORDERING AND SUPPLYING GOODS AND SERVICES

► THE PROCESS AND THE DOCUMENTS

Trading organizations will be dependent on buying and selling goods in order to make a profit, and the whole administrative function of the organization will revolve around this process.

It is most unusual for an organization not to need to order goods and services. Even non-profit-making organizations that do not trade themselves, eg Local Government Departments, voluntary agencies, will need to purchase office equipment and materials, the services of maintenance contractors and professional people such as accountants from time to time. They may require leaflets printing and these will have to be ordered and paid for.

The three departments directly concerned with the process of ordering and supplying goods and services will be the purchasing department, the sales department and the accounts department, but all other departments will have an equally important role to play. For example, production department to ensure that you have the goods available to sell; stores department to receive and despatch goods; personnel to ensure that the staff are available to do the work. The telephonist must make sure that telephone enquiries are handled efficiently and the mail room must ensure that documents reach their destination. This process illustrates how closely all departments and staff need to work together and the importance of good business relationships with colleagues and, of course, the customer/client.

Small items may be purchased with petty cash, but it is more usual for organizations to order goods on credit. This means that both the purchaser and supplier must keep a written record of goods that have been ordered, supplied and paid for. All organizations will have their own procedure and documents used for buying and selling goods, but there is a standard process that most organizations will follow and though the design of documents may vary the basic information given will remain the same. This process begins with an initial request for goods/services and ends when payment is made. Figure 6.1 outlines the process of ordering and supplying goods and the flow of documents between the purchaser and supplier. These documents will be looked at more closely.

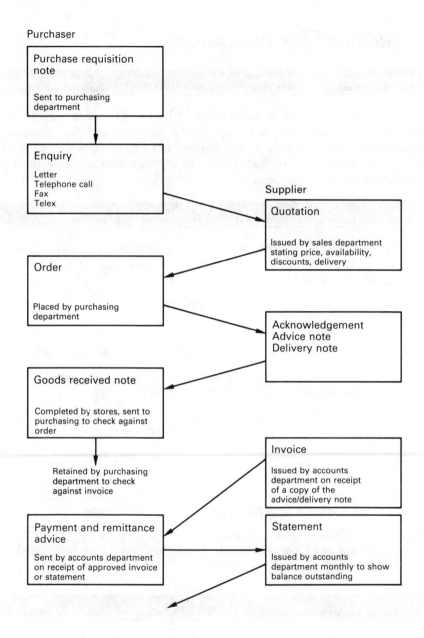

Purchaser

Purchase requisition note

Sent to purchasing department

Enquiry

Letter
Telephone call
Fax
Telex

Supplier

Quotation

Issued by sales department stating price, availability, discounts, delivery

Order

Placed by purchasing department

Acknowledgement Advice note Delivery note

Goods received note

Completed by stores, sent to purchasing to check against order

Retained by purchasing department to check against invoice

Invoice

Issued by accounts department on receipt of a copy of the advice/delivery note

Payment and remittance advice

Sent by accounts department on receipt of approved invoice or statement

Statement

Issued by accounts department monthly to show balance outstanding

Figure 6.1 *Outline of ordering and supplying goods*

► ENQUIRIES AND QUOTATIONS

Purchase requisition

The purchase requisition is usually signed by an authorized person. This document, like the one shown in Figure 6.2, instructs the purchasing department to order goods. If a supplier is not known then it is up to the purchasing department to find a suitable supplier who will give the best price/terms for the goods required.

Enquiry

If a supplier is not known then the purchasing department will have to make enquiries to see who can supply the goods. The following will be taken in to account when choosing a supplier:

1 The exact goods required can be supplied.

2 Price.

3 Delivery: whether the goods can be delivered immediately or not.

4 Carriage: how much will it cost for the goods to be transported and who will pay for this, the supplier or the purchaser?

Often the purchasing department will already have on file suppliers' catalogues and price lists, but if not the purchaser will obtain this information by sending a letter (this may be a standard form), making a telephone call, sending a fax or Telex, even using the electronic mail-box if both companies have the facility for this. Suppliers' details will be found from Trade directories, Yellow Pages, advertisements. Normally the same enquiry will be sent to several suppliers, so that a comparison can be made.

Figure 6.3 overleaf is an example of a typical letter of enquiry. If a word-processing package is available, a standard letter may be created and the details amended for each supplier.

Quotation

The supplier will respond to the letter of enquiry by giving a quotation that may be verbal or in written form. Obviously the supplier wishes to create a good impression, for this could possibly lead to additional business and all the guidelines on communicating in business as given in Section 2 must be

SHEPPERTON INDUSTRIES PLC

GHEPPERTON HOUGE
APPELTON INDUSTRIAL ESTATE   WA3 2BP

PURCHASE REQUISITION

From: .....A. WOOD.............   Requisition no: ...3.4.2.......

                                        Date: ....12.-.3.-.9*.........
Dept: ...STORES.............

[Supplier   ]

Not known

[   ]

Please order the following:

Qty	Description	Comments
100	Fluorescent Tubes	4ft 40 watt
250	Fluorescent Tubes	6ft 75 watt
200	Fluorescent Tubes	8ft 125 watt

Signature a.E..Wood...   Authorized by ...T. Barker......
                             Position Stores, Supervisor...

Figure 6.2 *Purchase requisition*

SHEPPERTON INDUSTRIES PLC
SHEPPERTON HOUSE
APPELTON INDUSTRIAL ESTATE   WA3 2BP

Our Ref: MJK/sk

13th March 199*

Ultrafine UK Ltd
Electrical Wholesalers
141 Mersey Road
BOOTLE
L20 8HG

Dear Sirs

As electrical contractors, we should be pleased if you would let us know if
you can supply the following light fittings together with your best terms and
conditions of delivery.

100   4ft 40 watt fluorescent tubes
250   6ft 75 watt fluorescent tubes
200   8ft 125 watt fluorescent tubes

We are also interested in your emergency lighting and illuminated signs and
would be grateful for your brochure and price list.

Yours faithfully

M J KENNEDY
Purchasing Manager

Figure 6.3 *Letter of enquiry*

100

ULTRAFINE UK LTD

ELECTRICAL WHOLESALERS

141 MERSEY ROAD, BOOTLE, l20 8HG

Your Ref: MJK/sk

Our Ref: 315/ACH/EP

16th March 199*

For the attention of M J Kennedy

Purchasing Manager
Shepperton Industries PLC
Shepperton House
Appelton Industrial Estate
WA3 2BP

Dear Mr Kennedy

In reply to your enquiry dated 13th March, we are pleased to advise that we can supply ex-stock the following items in white, cool white or natural:

Ref FT4.40W   4ft 40 watt fluorescent tubes @ £2.60 each + VAT
Ref FT6.75W   6ft 75 watt fluorescent tubes @ £3.00 each + VAT
Ref FT8.125W   8ft 125 watt fluorescent tubes @ £3.60 each + VAT

Carriage paid
Terms 2 1/2% 30 days
      20% Trade discount

We enclose information on our security lighting products, in particular emergency lighting and illuminated signs as requested, and our representative will contact you in a few days regarding this.

We look forward to receiving your order, which will receive our prompt attention.

Yours sincerely

A C Hart (Mrs)
Sales Manager

Enc

Figure 6.4 *Quotation*

101

followed. A quotation will state details of the goods to be supplied, the price, whether discounts are offered, delivery time, and whether carriage will be paid by the supplier or purchaser.

Discounts

The following discounts are frequently given.

Cash discount This is an incentive for prompt payment. It does not mean that payment must be made in coins and notes, but must be made within a stated period of time for the discount to be allowable.

Trade discount This is an incentive for people in the same trade to buy in bulk. This allows them to make extra profit when they sell the goods again. Figure 6.4 is an example of a quotation that includes a 20 per cent trade discount.

▶ MAKING AND RECEIVING THE ORDER

Raising an order

The purchaser will select the best quotation, and from this quotation raise an order. This is usually done on a specially printed form, the forms being numbered consecutively with an order number. Figure 6.5 is an example of a completed order form. The order number is very important because this shows that the order is official and it will be the reference number used on all subsequent documentation. Orders may be placed by telephone, providing an order number is quoted, but usually telephone orders are then confirmed in writing.

Action by the purchaser

1 The purchaser will send the order form to the supplier.

2 A copy will be kept for the purchasing department's records.

3 A copy will often be sent to the person/department requesting the goods.

Action by the supplier

On receiving the order form the supplier will check the goods are in stock and organize the following paper work.

1 Send the customer an **acknowledgement** of the order as a letter or pre-printed form. Many organizations do not send an acknowledgement,

SHEPPERTON INDUSTRIES PLC
SHEPPERTON HOUSE
APPELTON INDUSTRIAL ESTATE   WA3 2BP

ORDER FORM

To: Ultrafine UK Ltd
    141 Mersey Road
    BOOTLE
    L20 8HG

Order no: L.28934/1

Date: 20th March 199*

Date required: ASAP

Delivery
address: Shepperton Industries PLC
          Shepperton House
          Unit 12
          Appelton Industrial Estate
          APPELTON

Please supply and deliver:

Qty	Description	Stock code	Price
100	4ft 40 watt fluorescent tubes	FT4.40W	£2.60 each
250	6ft 75 watt fluorescent tubes	FT6.75W	£3.00 each
200	8ft 125 watt fluorescent tubes	FT8.125W	£3.60 each

Terms as per your quotation Ref: 315/ACH/EP

All invoices and statements to Head Office.
For conditions of purchase see over.
No goods accepted unless against official order no.

Signed ...*M. S. Kennedy*.................

Position ..*PURCHASING...MANAGER*.......

Figure 6.5 *Completed order form*

but it can be a useful document, particularly if goods are not in stock as it informs the customer that the order has been received and is being actioned.

2   Raise an **advice note** to inform the customer when and how the goods will be arriving. This is a very similar document to the delivery note and some organizations actually use a copy of the delivery note. The advice note is a useful document for the customer, as arrangements can be made for receiving the goods (ie sufficient warehouse space and staff to handle the delivery). Some organizations only use an advice note if the goods are not being despatched by the organization's own transport.

3   Raise a **delivery note** to be given to the transport department. This is sent with the goods, signed by the buyer and given back to the delivery driver as proof of delivery.

4   A copy of the order will be kept for the sales department's records.

5   A copy of the order together with the advice note and delivery note will be sent to accounts. Figure 6.6 is an example of a delivery note.

Goods received note

On receiving the goods, the purchaser will sign the delivery note and may keep a copy of this to use as a **goods received note**. Alternatively, a goods received book or note (Figure 6.7) may be completed. This shows exactly what goods have been received and the condition of them.

Action by purchaser

1   A copy is sent to the purchasing department to check against the order. It is then retained until the invoice is received. Any discrepancies or damages will be reported to the supplier.

2   A copy will be sent to the person responsible for the stock, so that stock records can be updated.

▶ INVOICING AND PAYMENT

Invoice

From the supplier's point of view this document is probably the most important, as this is the document requesting payment: 'the bill'. The

No. 000739

DELIVERY NOTE

From   Ultrafine UK Ltd   Delivery   Shepperton Industries PLC
        141 Mersey Road   address: Shepperton House
        BOOTLE   Appelton Industrial Estate
        L20 8HG   APPELTON

Despatch depot: Bootle   Order no: L.28934/1

Despatch date: 28th March 199*

Quantity   Goods
_____

100   4ft 40 watt fluorescent tubes
250   6ft 75 watt fluorescent tubes
200   8ft 125 watt fluorescent tubes

RECEIVED BY:..D. hangbury....   DATE:...1st April 9*...

POSITION ....Storeman..........

Figure 6.6 Delivery note

SHEPPERTON INDUSTRIES PLC
GOODS RECEIVED NOTE

Supplier: [   ]   Date: 1st April 9*

Ultrafine

[   ]   Order no: L.28934/.1

Quantity	Goods	Condition on delivery
100	4' Tubes	All O.K
250	6' Tubes	
200	8' Tubes	

Comments ....

Received By: R. Langbury

Position: Storeman

Figure 6.7 *Goods received note*

accounts department issues an invoice to the purchaser when they receive a copy of the advice note or delivery note, showing that the goods have been despatched.

Invoices may be handwritten, typewritten (as shown in Figure 6.8) or produced using a computer package. As well as producing an invoice the computer package will update the sales ledger (customer's account) and produce a statement of the account when required. It will also reduce the stock level on the stock record cards.

ULTRAFINE UK LTD

INVOICE N.º 2485

Comp Code: SHEP

Date: 2.4.9*

VAT Reg. No. 348

┌─────────────────────────┐ ┌─────────────────────────┐

Invoice address: **Delivery address:**

Shepperton Industries PLC
Shepperton House
Unit 12   As invoice address
Appelton Ind. Estate
Appelton
WA3 2BP

└─────────────────────────┘ └─────────────────────────┘

Customer's Order No. L 28934/1 Our Ref. 315/ACH/EP Date Shipped 1/4/9* Shipped via Own transport

Quantity Ordered	Sent	Description	Unit Price	Amount
100	100	FT4.40 W 4ft 40 W fluorescent tubes, white	2.60	260.00
250	250	FT6. 75 W 6ft 75 W fluorescent tubes, white	3.00	750.00
200	200	FT8.125 W 8ft 125 W fluorescent tubes, white	3.60	720.00
		Total goods		1730.00
		Less 20% Trade Discount		346.00
		Net value of goods		1384.00
		Carriage		– —
		+ VAT @ 17½%		236.14
		Terms 2½%/30 days = £34.60		
		Total amount due £		1620.14

Please remit to
  Accounts Dept, Ultrafine UK Ltd, 141 Mersey Road, Bootle, L20 8HG
  Bank details: Royal Bank of Scotland, Bootle Branch, A/c No. 0028106

Figure 6.8 *Invoice*

Note:

You will see from this invoice that the VAT is calculated on the assumption that the customer will take the cash discount of £34.60 making the overall total due £1585.54 (ie, £1384 − £34.60 = £1349.4; VAT 17½% of 1349.4 = £236.14).

Action by supplier

1 The top copy will be sent to the purchaser.

2 A copy will be kept by the accounts department to update the sales account (credit entry) and customer's account (debit entry).

3 A copy will be sent to the sales department for their records.

Action by purchaser

1 On receiving the invoice, the purchasing department will check it against the order and delivery note/goods received note to check:

a The correct goods have been invoiced, ie quantity and price.

b The date is correct.

c The calculations are correct.

d The VAT is correct.

Only if an organization is registered for VAT can they charge VAT. Look for their VAT registration number on the invoice. If the invoice is correct it will be passed to accounts.

2 On receiving the invoice the accounts department will update the purchases account (debit entry) and purchase ledger or supplier's account (credit entry).

3 The accounts department will then be responsible for paying the invoice.

Note:

If the invoice is incorrect, then the supplier should be informed. The invoice can be corrected by the supplier issuing one of the following.

A **Credit note**: given to correct an overcharge or to give a refund if goods are faulty, or not as requested. The amount of the credit note is then deducted from the invoice. Traditionally printed in red.

A **Debit note**: given if the purchaser has been undercharged. This is a request for additional payment.

Statement

This is sent to the purchaser by the supplier at the end of each month or quarter. It shows all purchases and payments, including credit and debit notes, during the period and the balance outstanding.

Action by the purchaser

1 The statement will be checked for accuracy against the purchase ledger (supplier's account).

2 The balance outstanding will then be paid.

Payment

Payment is usually by cheque or BACS (see Section 7). Many organizations now choose to pay by BACS, so bank details should be printed on the invoice. Payment should be accompanied by a remittance advice (see Figure 6.9), which is simply a letter or note to show what the payment is for.

REMITTANCE ADVICE

From: Shepperton Industries PLC   Date: 30th April 199*
            Shepperton House
            Appelton Industrial Estate
            WA3 2BP

To: Ultrafine UK Ltd
            Electrical Wholesalers
            141 Mersey Road
            Bootle
            L20 8HG

Date	Invoice No.	Value	Method of payment
02.04.9*	2485	£1585.54	Cheque

Total remittance £1585.54

Figure 6.9 *Remittance advice*

Action by the purchaser

1 The purchase ledger will be updated (debit entry).

2 The cash book will be updated (credit entry).

Action by the supplier

1 The payment will be checked against the sales ledger (customer's account) to see that it is correct.

2 The money will be deposited at the bank (see Section 7).

3 The sales ledger will be updated (credit entry).

4 The cash book will be updated (debit entry).

> **IMPORTANT** *All copies of documents must be filed appropriately so that they can be found easily when required. Time must not be wasted by departments in processing the documents, or payments will be delayed.*

Glossary of terms used in buying and selling

Carriage Method of delivery/transport.

Carriage forward Delivery will be charged to the purchaser.

Carriage paid Delivery will be paid for by the supplier.

COD Cash on delivery. New customers or customers with a poor payment record may be asked to pay for the goods on delivery.

Credit control It is important for an organization that is offering credit to a customer, that they check the customer's ability to pay. This is usually done by obtaining a banker's reference or a reference from another organization that the company have traded with. It is also important for an accounts department to have a credit control system for following up overdue accounts. Money outstanding will be requested by telephone and/or letter, if the money is not received within a reasonable period of time then the supplier may take legal action.

Ex-stock The goods are in stock for immediate delivery.

NCR forms Documents requiring multiple copies are often printed on NCR (meaning no carbon required) paper so that the details entered on the top copy will automatically be duplicated. The copies will often be on different coloured paper to assist in distribution.

Pro-forma invoice Used where payment is required before goods can be sent or when goods are sold **cash on delivery**. Often used for new customers, where their creditworthiness is not known. Also sent with goods on approval, to show the customer the amount to be paid should they decide to keep the goods.

Shipped Another term for carriage.

Tax point This is the date on which VAT is charged and will be the date of the invoice.

Trade Descriptions Act 1968 Anyone selling goods or providing services (not private sales) is under a legal obligation to avoid making false or misleading statements about them to prospective customers. If it is felt by the customer that the supplier is in breach of this act, a complaint can be made to the trading standards department at the local council. They will enforce the act and if there is a case prosecute the supplier.

FINANCIAL RECORD KEEPING

Businesses normally operate for one purpose and that is to make money or **profit** by buying and selling goods/services. You may work for an organization whose primary aim is not to make money, but to offer a service to the public, eg a local authority, a health authority, a library, a voluntary organization. All these non-profit-making organizations will still have to handle money and whether you are talking about £5 or £5 million all organizations must keep records of the money they have spent and received, so that at any time they can see exactly how much money they have. It would therefore be impossible to run an organization efficiently without financial record keeping. Think how confused you become if you do not keep a note of money you deposit and withdraw from your bank account; when you finally get a statement from the bank it might be a pleasant or unpleasant surprise.

By law any profit-making organization must keep records so that the Government can see how much tax the organization owes to them from the money they have made. It is also necessary to keep records so that the owners of the company, who may or may not be directly involved in running the company, can see how successful or unsuccessful it has been.

► COMPANY ACCOUNTS

Organizations record money coming in and money going out by keeping accounts or 'books' into which all financial transactions are entered. These may be kept manually or by using a computer package (see Section 8).

As an example imagine a company that is formed with £10 000 loaned to the company by the owner, A Woods. This money would be the company's capital. The company would open a bank account and pay this money in, keeping a financial record of it as shown in Figure 7.1.

Double-entry bookkeeping

Note that there are two sides to the account, named Dr (short for debit) meaning money received or owed to the company and Cr (short for credit)

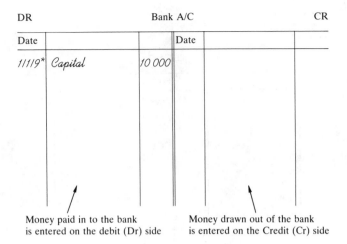

DR	Bank A/C		CR
Date		Date	
1/1/9* Capital	10 000		

Money paid in to the bank
is entered on the debit (Dr) side

Money drawn out of the bank
is entered on the Credit (Cr) side

Figure 7.1 *Financial record*

meaning money paid out or owed by the company. This £10 000 is placed on the left of the account or Dr side as it is money the company has received.

However, this money is a loan, which means that at some stage it must be paid back to the owner and this must be shown in the accounts. Any entry in an account will always have a double, like a mirror image, appearing in the company's books on the opposite side. If you have received money, then you must show where it has come from and, similarly, if you have paid out money, then you must show what you have bought. This is called double-entry bookkeeping.

In this case the loan money will also appear in a capital account on the credit side, because it is money owed by the company (see Figure 7.2).

We now have the double entry: the money is in the bank, but it is also shown as loan capital which must be paid back. This principle will continue every time money is received or spent. Let us see what would happen if the company now bought stock of value £750 by cheque. This means money would be taken out of the bank account as shown in Figure 7.3 and the double entry would appear in the purchases account to show that we have bought goods to the value of £750. These goods are an **asset** to the company, because they can be sold at a later date and therefore purchases are always entered on the debit side of the purchases account (Figure 7.4).

If we then found that some of the goods we purchased were faulty and returned them, receiving £50 back from the supplier as a refund, the entries would be reversed. We would reduce the stock we have purchased by making

DR			Capital A/C		CR
Date			Date		
			1/1/9*	Bank	10 000

Figure 7.2 *Double-entry record*

DR			Bank A/C		CR
Date			Date		
1/1/9*	Capital	10 000	2/1/9*	Purchases	750

Figure 7.3 *Credit bank account with money spent on purchases*

DR   Purchases A/C   CR

Date			Date		
2/1/9*	Bank	750			

Figure 7.4 *Debit purchases*

DR   Purchases A/C   CR   DR   Bank A/C   CR

Date			Date			Date			Date		
2/1/9*	Bank	750	4/1/9*	Returns	50	1/1/9*	Capital	10 000	2/1/9*	Purchases	750
						4/1/9*	Purchase Returns	50			

Figure 7.5 *Purchases account and bank account*

DR	Sales A/C		CR	DR		Bank A/C		CR
Date		Date		Date			Date	
		5/1/19* Bank	100	1/1/19* Capital	10 000		2/1/19* Purchases	750
				4/1/19* Purchase returns	50			
				5/1/19* Sales	100			

Figure 7.6 *Sales account and bank account*

a credit entry in the purchases account and pay the £50 received in to the bank as a debit entry (Figure 7.5).

If we now sell goods for cash and receive £100 that we pay in to the bank then we would debit the bank account with the money paid in. We would then credit our sales account, because once goods have been sold they are no longer of value to the company (see Figure 7.6).

Buying and selling goods on credit

In reality most organizations buy and sell goods and services on credit. The purchaser will send an order requesting goods and the supplier will send the purchaser an invoice (bill) when the goods have been supplied (see Section 6). Because with most trading organizations this would involve numerous entries in the purchases and sales account, to simplify the procedure all entries are first made in a purchases day book or sales day book. The information is then transferred to the purchases and sales account weekly or monthly.

Purchases day book

The purchaser will enter all invoices (bills) received in a purchases day book, which will show **what has been purchased** under separate headings (see Figure 7.7).

At the end of a week or month the total will be transferred to the debit of the purchasing account. Each supplier will have their own account and the amount of each invoice will be entered on the credit side as this is money owed to the supplier (see Figure 7.8).

Purchases Day Book

Date	Supplier	Inv. No.	Total	Stock	Equipment	Advertising	VAT
7/1/9*	J Parker & Co	00214	£514	437.45			76.55
8/1/9*	AA Adverts	02031	£220			187.23	32.77
22/1/9*	Foss Chemicals	2145	·£301	256.17			44.83
			£1035	£693.62		£187.23	£154.15

Figure 7.7 *Purchases day book*

DR	Purchases A/C		CR	DR	J Parker & Co.		CR
Date		Date		Date		Date	
31/1/9* PDB	1035					7/1/9* Purchases	514

Figure 7.8 *Purchases account and J Parker & Co.*

Sales day book

The supplier will enter all invoices (bills) raised in a sales day book (Figure 7.9), which will show **who goods have been sold to**.

Sales Day Book

Date	Invoice No.	Customer	Net Amount	Tax Amount
4/1/9*	000100	A T Dalzell	520.00	91.00
8/1/9*	000101	A + B Electrics	201.05	35.18
20/1/9*	000102	Alarm Electrics	50.25	8.79
21/1/9*	000103	J B Fittings	304.00	53.20
			1075.30	188.17

Figure 7.9 *Sales day book*

At the end of a week or month the total will be transferred to the credit of the sales account. Each customer will have their own account and the amount of the invoice will be entered on the debit side as this is money they owe to us as the supplier (see Figure 7.10).

DR		Sales A/C		CR	Dr		A T Dalzell		Cr
Date		Date			Date		Date		
		3/1/19* S.D.B.	1075.30		4/1/19* Sales	520.00			

Figure 7.10 *Sales account and A. T. Dalzell*

Glossary of bookkeeping terms

Balance   The difference between debits and credits: a figure that will make both sides of the account equal to the same amount.

Cash book   In most organizations the cash book combines the cash and bank account together in one book. Figure 7.11 shows the entries we have made so far in the bank account. The cash side of the account tends to be rarely used, as most cash purchases are entered in the petty cash book (see page 120). However, some organizations will want to show cash transactions in the cash

Dr				Cash Book					Cr
Date	Details	Cash	Bank	Date	Details			Cash	Bank
1/1/19*	Capital		10 000	2/1/19*	Purchases				750
4/1/19*	Purchase returns		50						
5/1/19*	Sales		100						

Figure 7.11 *Cash book showing bank account entries*

book, for example if cash is withdrawn from the bank to pay wages. The cash book would then be as shown in Figure 7.12. To balance the cash book: Total the debt column for cash and the debit column for bank. Next total the credit column for cash and the credit column for bank. The difference between the total on the debit and the total on the credit will be the balance, insert this balance to make the totals the same. Bring forward whatever balance remains for the next accounting period. If money is remaining, this will be a debit entry. Balance off the account as shown in Figure 7.13.

Dr				Cash Book				Cr
Date	Details	Cash	Bank	Date	Details	Cash	Bank
1/1/9*	Capital		10 000	2/1/9*	Purchases		750
4/1/9*	Purchase returns		50	10/1/9*	Cash		500 ^{a}
5/1/9*	Sales		100	11/1/9*	Wages	500 ^{c}	
10/1/9*	Bank	500 ^{b}					

^{a} = Cash withdrawn from the Bank
^{b} = Cash paid in to cash A/c.
^{c} = Cash withdrawn from cash a/c to pay wages

Figure 7.12 *Cash book showing cash transactions*

Dr				Cash Book				Cr
Date	Details	Cash	Bank	Date	Details	Cash	Bank
1/1/9*	Capital		10 000	2/1/9*	Purchases		750
4/1/9*	Purchase returns		50	10/1/9*	Cash		500
5/1/9*	Sales		100	11/1/9*	Wages	500	
10/1/9*	Bank	500		31/1/9*	Balances c/f		8 900
		500	10 150			500	10 150
1/2/9*	Balances b/f		8 900				

c/f = Carried forward
b/f = Brought forward

Figure 7.13 *Cash book showing balancing*

Credit (CR)   Money paid out or owed by the company.

Creditor   Someone the company owes money to.

Debit (DR)   Money received by or owed to the company.

Debtor   Someone who owes money to the company.

Double-entry bookkeeping   For any debit entry there must also be a credit to make the books balance.

Nominal or general ledger   Contains all accounts of a double-entry system, other than purchases and sales.

Purchases day book   A record of all invoices received. It is not part of the double-entry system. The double-entry is the subsequent entry in the purchases account/supplier's account.

Purchase or bought ledger   This contains all suppliers' accounts (creditors).

Sales day book   A record of all invoices sent to customers/clients. It is not part of the double-entry system. The double-entry is the subsequent entry in the sales account/customer's account.

Sales ledger   This contains all customers/clients accounts (debtors).

► PETTY CASH

The word **petty** means small or minor and this is exactly what a sum of money is set aside to pay for. These are minor items of expenditure where the use of a cheque or invoice would be impractical, for example cleaning materials, toilet rolls, coffee, flowers, the window cleaner, stamps, items of stationery, etc. (Often stationery is ordered from a supplier in bulk, but in small companies or in an emergency, items may be purchased with money from petty cash.)

Petty cash book

Records have to be kept to ensure that the cash is used for the correct purpose. The most common method of recording the use of petty cash is in a petty cash book using **the imprest system**. The imprest is the amount of money that is set aside for petty cash and this has to be topped up as the money is spent.

Where does the sum of money known as the imprest for petty cash come from? This must be shown in the organization's accounts. If the company draws £100 from the bank to use for petty cash the financial records shown in Figure 7.14 would be kept.

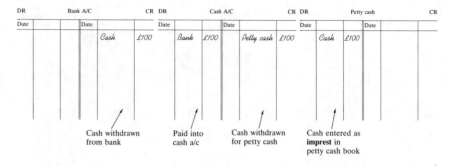

Figure 7.14 *Bank account/cash account/petty cash*

Every time petty cash is spent, a petty cash voucher is completed giving details of the purchase and signed by someone authorized to do so. A completed voucher is shown in Figure 7.15. Any time that a check is made, the sum of the cash and vouchers in the cash box should equal the initial imprest.

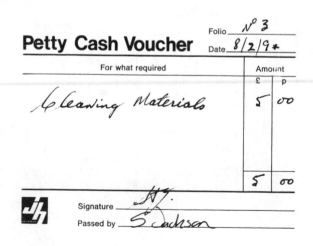

Figure 7.15 *Petty cash voucher*

These petty cash vouchers are then used to complete the petty cash book. As you will see from the example given (Figure 7.16 overleaf), the account is drawn up with columns to show how the money is spent; these are called

Petty Cash

Receipts	Date	Details	Voucher No.	Total Payment	Postage	Travel	Stationery	Office Expenses	Hospitality	VAT
50 00	Feb 1	Imprest from cashier								
	Feb 3	Stamps	1	4 76	4 76					
	Feb 1	Coffee	2	1 95					1 95	0 74
	Feb 8	Cleaning materials	3	5 00				5 00		
	Feb 10	Envelopes	4	1 10			2 10			0 31
	Feb 13	Taxi fare	5	4 60		4 60				
	Feb 19	Milk	6	3 70					3 70	
	Feb 22	Lunch for visitors	7	21 00					21 00	3 13
		Total spent		43 11	4 76	4 60	2 10	5 00	26 65	4 18
		Balance c/f		6 89						
50 00				50 00						
6 89	mar 1	Balance b/f								
43 11	Mar 1	Imprest from cashier								

This sum of money will top up the imprest to its original amount.

The balance is the sum of money remaining after all expenditure. This figure will make the total on each side the same.

Payments are analysed to show a breakdown of expenditure. If the payment includes VAT, this must be separated out in the analysis columns.

Figure 7.16 Petty cash book

analysis columns. This is to enable you to see at the end of the week or month how much has been spent on different items, eg travel, stationery. Each of these items should then have their own account in the purchase ledger, where a debit entry will be made. This is usually done by the cashier or accounts department.

▶ POSTAGE BOOK

If we use petty cash to buy stamps, it is highly likely that we will keep a postage book to show how the stamps have been used and what value of postage we have left. Though this record is not required by law and serves no purpose other than to show the amount of postage used, it is still drawn up using the same principles of bookkeeping.

If we receive £50 from petty cash to buy stamps, this £50 would appear on the left or debit side of the postage book as shown in Figure 7.17.

Postage Book				
Stamps bought	Date	Name and town	Stamps used	Details
50.00	1.5.9*	Brimley's, Liverpool	0.18	
		Foss, Liverpool	0.18	
		P. Wilson, Sheffield	0.24	
		S. Barker, Wolverhampton	0.18	
		Circular to suppliers	1.80	10 × 2nd class
		L. Fittings, Stroud	0.64	240g 1st class
		T. Simmons, Oxford	0.34	125g 2nd class
			3.56	
		Balance c/f	46.44	
50.00			50.00	
46.44	2.5.9*	Balance b/f		
c/f = carried forward				
b/f = brought forward				

Figure 7.17 *Postage book*

► VALUE ADDED TAX

Value added tax (VAT) is charged to the buyer on the selling price of goods and services. This means that any item you purchase will include VAT at the current rate of 17½% (the rate of VAT is set by the Government), unless the goods/services are zero-rated and therefore exempt from VAT, for example:

- Food items, but not once they are prepared and offered for sale in a restaurant; this then becomes a service.
- Children's clothes.
- Postage.
- Travel fares.
- Donations to charity.
- Books.

Before VAT can be charged the individual or company providing the goods/services has to be registered for VAT. You will see a VAT registration number on their bill. Any individual/company whose sales exceed the limit set by the Government must be registered for VAT or they are liable to a 'fine'. The Government department responsible for collection of VAT is HM Customs and Excise. Money collected for VAT is usually paid to the Tax Office three-monthly.

Any organization registered to charge VAT can also reclaim the VAT that they are charged on any business purchases/expenses.

> *Note*:
> In a three-month period a company sells goods and the total VAT on the goods sold amounts to **£574**.
> In the same period the company purchases goods and the total VAT on the goods purchased amounts to **£421**.
> The company only needs to pay the difference, **£153**, to the tax office when the tax return is due.

It is therefore important that an organization keeps an accurate record of the amount of VAT paid and received in a VAT account. You will see that in the example of a petty cash account the VAT is calculated and shown in an analysis column, the total figure for VAT will then be transferred to the VAT account.

How to calculate VAT

Find out the VAT rate — currently 17½%. To charge VAT simply add 17½% to the selling price of the goods/services:

Goods   = £150
+ VAT @ 17½%   = £26.25 (150 × 17.5%)
Total price of goods= £176.25

To calculate how much VAT has been paid, divide the total amount by 1.175.

Goods   = £172.50 including VAT
Divide by 1.175   = £146.81
VAT will be the difference = £25.69

▶ RECEIVING AND MAKING PAYMENTS

Every time we receive or make payments the ledgers (accounts) will have to
be updated. Remember if we receive money in settlement of customers'
accounts, this will debit our bank account and credit the sales ledger. If we
pay our suppliers, this will credit our bank account and debit the purchase
ledger.

An organization will have to make payments for various items, for example:

- Goods received.
- Wages and salaries.
- Bills for maintenance work.
- Expense claims.
- HM Customs and Excise (tax).
- Insurance.
- Auditor's fees.
- Garage bills.

Payment is usually made accompanied by a **remittance advice**. This is simply a
letter or pre-printed form that explains what the payment is for (see Section
6).

Methods of payment

An organization may use the following methods of payment.

Cash

This is not a common method of payment in business for settling accounts.
Petty cash is used to purchase minor items, and wages/expense claims may be
paid in cash. To make payments by cash, you will probably have to
withdraw the cash from the bank and complete a withdrawal slip.

A CASH ANALYSIS

Name	Emp. No.	Details	Net amt.	£20	£10	£5	£1	50p	20p	10p	5p	2p	1p
J. Bird	00214	Wages	£148.60	5	4	1	3	1		1			
S. Harper	00056	Wages	£129.20	5	2	1	4		1				
A. Kirk	01426	Expenses	£31.14		3		1			1		2	
Total notes and coins				10	9	2	8	1	1	2		2	
Total value			£308.94	£200	£90	£10	£8	£0.50	£0.20	£0.20	–	£0.04	–

Figure 7.18 *A cash analysis*

> **THINK!** *Before you withdraw the money decide how you would like the cash. Will £20 notes be practical or do you require a variety of notes and coins?*

If you are paying people expenses or wages then it is highly unlikely that you will just require notes to make up the exact amount. Prepare a **cash analysis** in advance, which will give you a breakdown of the money you require (see for example Figure 7.18).

Then complete the withdrawal slip as shown in Figure 7.19.

Note:
If withdrawing money from a current account, then it is usual to write a cheque with the words 'pay cash'.

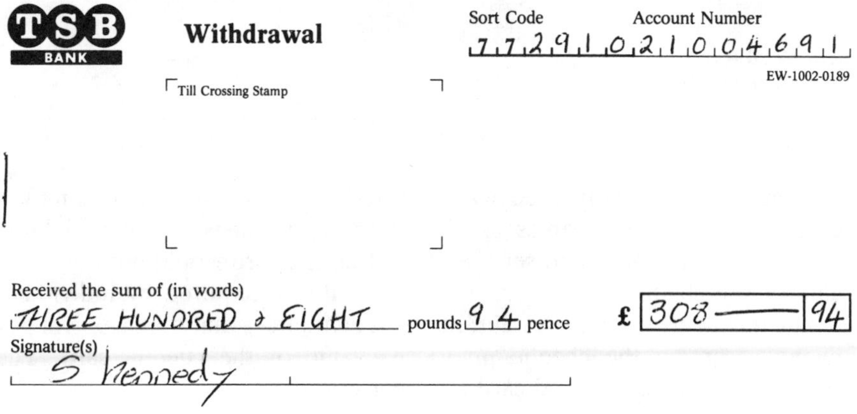
TSB BANK
Withdrawal
Sort Code 77-29-10 Account Number 21004691
EW-1002-0189
Till Crossing Stamp
Received the sum of (in words)
THREE HUNDRED & EIGHT pounds 94 pence £ 308—94
Signature(s)
S Kennedy

Figure 7.19 *Withdrawal slip*
(Reproduced by kind permission of TSB)

Cheque

A cheque is a written instruction to the bank to pay the person named on the cheque a stated sum of money from the writer's bank account. Before you can write cheques you therefore need to have a current account at a bank and as most organizations do, this is a very common method of payment. A cheque is valid for six months from the date it has been written. Cheques may be written out by hand, but are now frequently printed out by computer as part of an accounting package. The cheque will still need to be signed.

Each part of the cheque must be completed correctly for the cheque to be valid. Most cheques are crossed, two vertical lines running through the middle of the cheque (Figure 7.20), which means that it must be paid into a bank account.

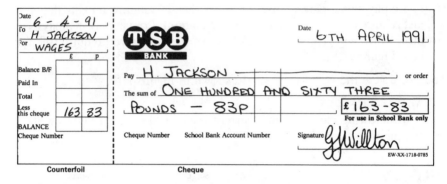

Figure 7.20 *A completed cheque*
(Reproduced by kind permission of TSB)

Cheque guarantee card

This card is not usually used by organizations in the settlement of their accounts, as most companies check the creditworthiness of their debtors before supplying goods and services and often the card would not cover the value of the cheque. However, the card would be required by individuals making payments in shops/restaurants, as it guarantees that the bank will pay anyone accepting the cheque up to the value of the cheque card. The signature on the cheque and card must correspond.

Postal orders

These are used by organizations as well as individuals, but they are not as common as cheques. They are particularly useful if the sender or receiver does not have a bank account. They can be easily purchased from the post office from 25p up to any value and are accepted in around 50 countries worldwide. They are valid for six months from the date of issue.

A postal order may be crossed by drawing two parallel lines vertically through it. This means it cannot be cashed at a post office and must be paid in to a bank account. A fee is charged for every postal order purchased and this varies according to the value, eg the fee on a postal order valued £10 is 60p. Once you have purchased the postal order, complete it as shown in Figure 7.21.

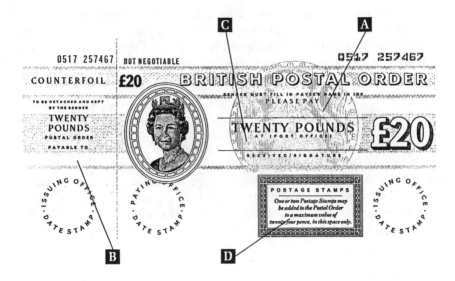

Figure 7.21 *A completed postal order*
(Reproduced by kind permission of The Post Office)

- Enter your own name and address on the reverse of the postal order in the space provided.
  It is important to fill out both sides.
- Your counter clerk may have given you one or two stamps in order to make your postal order up to the exact amount you require. Stick the stamps in the space provided (D).
- Enter the name of the person or company to whom you are sending the postal order on both the postal order (A) and the counterfoil (B).
- If you know the name of the post office or town where the postal order is to be cashed, enter the details (C). If you don't then leave it blank.

Credit transfer: Banker's Automated Clearing Service

This system (abbreviation: BACS) enables an organization to pay creditors without having to send each creditor a cheque. The bank will supply a credit transfer form that must be completed with the name of each creditor, the creditor's bank, branch and account number. It may be necessary to find out these details from the creditor first. The organization will then write one cheque to cover the complete amount to the bank and the bank will transfer the amount of money stated from your bank account to the creditor's bank account. Usually the organization will send the creditor a remittance advice to inform them that the money is being paid by BACS. This is also a very useful method of paying salaries. The money is paid directly into the employee's bank account.

Credit cards

A credit card offers credit to the card holder, which means that goods and services may be purchased and paid for later, such cards being Access, Barclaycard, Visa. Widely used by individuals, but not commonly used by organizations. However, sales representatives or other employees may use credit cards to pay for their expenses, eg petrol and then claim the money back from the organization at a later stage using the sales voucher, which has to be completed in duplicate at the time of purchase and the top copy handed to the customer. This serves as proof of purchase as the voucher itemizes the purchases.

Charge cards

These cards are commonly used by organizations for paying 'out of office expenses', particularly as they are widely accepted abroad. The companies operating the charge card service (like American Express, Diner's) require a subscription to cover administrative costs and payment in full at the end of the month. No further credit time is allowed. However, they are convenient and avoid having to carry large sums of cash. Again the sales voucher receipts can be used to claim back expenses.

Receiving payments

If you are responsible for receiving payments, always check the following.

1 The value of payment is correct (in whatever form the payment is made).

2 *Cheques/postal orders are completed correctly*, otherwise they will be invalid. Check the name of payee, date, signature, and that the sum of money in figures and words on the cheque is the same. If any alterations have been made then these should be initialled by the person who has signed the cheque.

3 *Credit cards*   There is much fraud regarding credit cards and you must carry out the following routine precautions.

   a On accepting a credit card you must fill in a sales voucher. Keep the card in your hand and ask the customer to sign the voucher. Check that the signature agrees with that on the card.

b Find out your organization's policy on checking the customer's credit limit. Most organizations will have a figure over which it will be necessary to ring the card company and ensure that the customer still has sufficient credit in hand to cover the purchase.

c Lists of stolen cards are sent to organizations that accept the cards of a particular card company. It is worth discreetly checking that the card does not appear on the list: sometimes there is a reward for discovering stolen cards.

d Make sure that you do not misplace the completed and signed sales voucher. This will be sent to the appropriate card company to obtain payment.

4 *Cash* Many organizations are now checking bank notes to see that they are not forgeries. Count the money carefully.

> **IMPORTANT** *Once you have received payment, it is necessary to deposit the money at the bank. As business bank accounts charge for transactions, your organization may have a strict policy on when to pay money in to the bank. Whatever the policy you will have to complete a paying-in slip (Figure 7.22).*

Security procedures for handling money

If you are working in the finance department or handling money as part of your job, you must be very conscious of security procedures to avoid theft. Your organization may have a clear policy on security with elaborate security equipment and security guards, but if there are no procedures/guidelines for handling cash, observe the following rules.

Cash in the office

Always ensure that any cash in the office is locked away. Use a steel cash box, but remember that these are very portable, so the cash box itself must be locked in a drawer or cupboard. Keep the key safe and ensure a duplicate is kept with a senior member of staff. Some cash boxes now have a digital combination lock (example; $\boxed{0}\boxed{9}\boxed{7}$) rather than a key.

If you are dealing with a large amount of money it is advisable for the organization to purchase a combination safe.

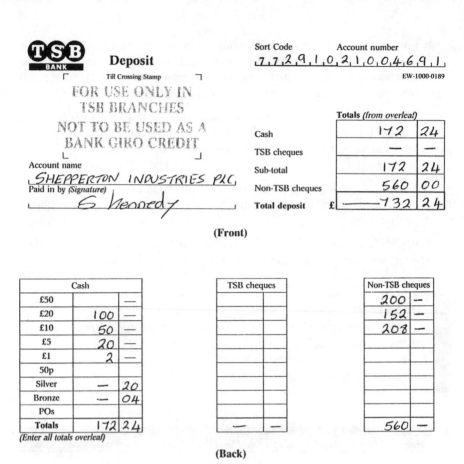

Figure 7.22 *A completed paying-in slip*
(Reproduced by kind permission of TSB)

Depositing/withdrawing cash from the bank

Where possible a closed vehicle should always be used for the transportation of moderate to large sums of money to and from the bank. The vehicle should be in good mechanical repair and preferably have an alarm fitted.

Alternatively, if on foot, it is best if two persons transport the money. The police recommend that one acts as an escort and walks a few yards behind the person carrying the money in order to raise the alarm if necessary. Another suggestion is that the money is divided between the two persons, thereby halving the risk.

If you are transporting money always be vigilant. Walk facing oncoming traffic and take the busy route, rather than a quiet one. If you regularly deposit/withdraw money from the bank then vary your route and/or the time of day.

Carry the money in a secure bag or case. If notes can be carried on the person, then this involves less risk to the money, but may be a greater risk to the employee.

Paying out wages

Ensure that wage packets are made up in a locked room, with only those employees responsible for making up the wages and a security guard (if employed) present.

When it is pay day, many organizations lock external doors to the building and pay wages through a purpose-built 'hatch'. Employees will be asked to sign for their wages and may be asked to provide identification. Again, if the organization has a security guard, they would usually be present.

> *THINK!* *Keep money in a safe place. Be careful where you keep keys to the cash box or safe. Ensure windows are closed in your absence. If you see a stranger in the building, ask if you can help them. Never leave a stranger/visitor alone in your office. Is everyone honest? Take proper precautions even with colleagues. Use your common sense. Your local crime prevention officer will always give advice on security matters: the telephone number is in your local phone book.*

► CALCULATING WAGES AND SALARIES

Every employee expects to earn a wage or salary for the job they do. A wage is a sum of money that is paid weekly. A salary is a sum of money that is paid monthly.

If you work for a small organization you may be responsible for calculating wages and salaries in addition to carrying out other duties. In a large organization, you may be employed in the accounts department as a wages clerk.

Wages and salaries may be prepared manually or by computer using a payroll package. If you know how to calculate wages manually this will give you a better understanding of how the computer package operates.

Rates of pay

The sum of money paid to employees may be calculated in various ways depending on the employee's job:

Flat rate

Most full-time office workers are paid a salary monthly. This is usually a flat rate, ie they are paid a sum of money each year that is divided by 12 and they receive $\frac{1}{12}$ each month. For example, a wages clerk who earns £7950 per year will receive £662.50 per month gross.

Hourly rate

Temporary office staff, part-time staff and workers whose jobs are too varied to be calculated on a flat rate basis are paid an hourly rate. It is important to keep an accurate record of the number of hours worked and this may involve the use of a time card, sometimes called a clock card (Figure 7.24). On arriving for duty employees put their time card in a clock machine that stamps the time of arrival on the card. On leaving the employee stamps the card again. At the end of the week, the wages clerk will total the hours worked and multiply the number of hours by the rate of pay per hour to give the gross wage.

A timesheet, like the one shown in Figure 7.23, may also be used for recording the number of hours worked. As this is completed by the employee, it usually has to be verified and signed by a senior member of staff.

Piece rate

Machinists and assembly workers are often paid for the number of items they produce and this is an incentive for workers to produce as many items as possible. Piece-work tickets have to be completed to show the number of items produced and again these need to be verified. The number is then multiplied by the rate of pay per piece to calculate the gross pay.

Commission

Some workers, particularly sales representatives, are paid purely commission. This means that they earn a percentage of all sales. Other companies may pay the representative a flat rate, in addition to commission.

TIMESHEET: Week Commencing Date.. 25/2/9*......................

		MON	TUE	WED	THUR	FRI	SAT	SUN	TOTAL
HOURS WORKED	Standard Hours	7	7	7	7	7			35
(EXCLUDE LUNCHBREAKS)	Overtime	1		2					3

NAME

H Jackson

EMPLOYEE NO.			
0	4	5	6

JOB   SIGNATURE

Finance clerk   *HJackson*

SUPERVISOR   *P. Davies*

OFFICE USE

F	STANDARD	O/TIME	BONUS
HOURS	35	3	—
PAY RATE	6.25	9.38	—
BILL RATE	218.75	28.14	—

246.89

Figure 7.23 *Timesheet*

Overtime

This is usually a 'higher' hourly rate and is paid for work carried out after normal working hours. The figure must be added onto the basic pay.

Flexi-time

Used in conjunction with other methods of payment, it simply allows employees to vary their arrival and departure times. Usually a specified block of time (core time) has to be worked by all staff, but then staff can choose how to make up their set number of hours per week, for example:

Working week = 35 hours
Core time = 11am–3pm (one hour for lunch)
Remaining hours may be made up between 7am and 7pm each day.

Time cards are usually required with flexi-time in order to keep an accurate record of the hours worked (see Figure 7.24).

NAME	D. T. Hart		No.		0221	
DEPT.	Stores		Week Ending		22.2.9*	
DAY	IN	OUT	IN	OUT	HOURS	
MON	0800	1200	1300	1700	8	
TUES	0802	1300	1400	1700	8	
WED	0759	1200	1300	1800	9	
THUR	0800	1205	1300	1700	8	
FRI	0800	1200	1302	1700	8	
SAT	0800	1200			4	
SUN						
TOTAL HOURS WORKED						
ORD. TIME	40	RATE	4.50	TOTAL	180.00	
O.TIME	5	RATE	6.75	TOTAL	33.75	
	GROSS WAGES			£ 213	P 75	

Figure 7.24 Clock card

Very few employees are paid a **gross** wage. By law deductions have to be made for Income Tax and National Insurance, if the employee earns over the lower earnings limit set by the Government. In addition the employee may choose to have money deducted for superannuation (pension) schemes, trade union subscriptions, social funds, etc. The figure that the employee takes home is then called **net pay**.

Calculating net pay

Ensure that you have the following:

- The employee's Tax Code No. and National Insurance No. (usually shown on a form P45 which the employee should have been given by their previous employer). The tax code is issued to the employee by the Inland Revenue and indicates (depending on personal circumstances) how much tax they are eligible to pay.
- Table A: Free Pay Table issued by the Inland Revenue.
- Tables B to D: Taxable Pay Tables issued by the Inland Revenue.
- National Insurance Contribution Tables issued by the DSS.

Step 1

Calculate the statutory deductions, ie tax and NI. Use a P11, deductions working sheet, available from the Inland Revenue. The Inland Revenue will give you full details on how to complete this, but the example shown in Figure 7.25 and notes 1–9 may be helpful.

1 Complete the employee's details from their P45. If there is no P45 use the emergency code 300L and give the employee a Coding Claim Form P15 to send to the tax office. Ask the employee to sign a P46 and send this to your tax office as soon as possible.

2 Complete column 2 for the relevant date with the gross pay figure. Remember the tax year starts on 1 April, so w/c 1 April is week 1.

3 Complete column 3. Add the figure in column 2 to the previous total in column 3 to give **total pay to date**.

4 Turn to Table A. Find the relevant week number. Look up the employee's code number and this will show the **total free pay** allowed to date. Enter this in column 4.

Deductions working sheet P11 (New)

Employee's name	JACKSON (in BLOCK letters)
Employee's surn.	JACKSON
First two forenames	HENRY
Employer's name	SHEPPERTON INDUSTRIES PLC
Tax District and reference	83/1604
National Insurance no.	XP 14 37 84 E
Date of birth in figures Day	Month	Year	18	8	50
Works no. etc	0456
Tax Code†	328
Amended code†	
Date of leaving in figures Day	Month	Year	
Week/Month no. in which applied	
Year to 5 April	19.1.1

National Insurance Contributions

Total of Employer's and Employee's Contributions payable 1a	Employee's contributions payable 1b	Employee's contributions at Contracted-out rate included in Col. 1b 1c	Statutory sick pay included in col. 2 1d
44 72	18 96	✓	✓
44 72	18 96	✓	✓

PAYE Income Tax

WEEK number	MONTH number	Pay in the week or month including statutory sick pay 2	Total pay to date 3	Total free pay to date as shown by Table A 4	Total taxable pay to date ⓐ 5	Total tax due to date as shown by Taxable Pay Tables 6	Tax deducted or refunded in the week or month Mark refunds "R" 7	For employer's use
1	1 April to 5 May	246 89	246 89	63 25	183 64	45 75	45 75	
2		246 89	493 78	126 50	361 28	91 75	46 00	
3								
4								
5	2 May to 5 June							
6								
7								
8								
9	3 June to 5 July							
10								
11								
12								
13								
14	4 July to 5 Aug							
15								
16								
17								
18	5 Aug to 5 Sept							
19								
20								
21								
22	6 Sept to 5 Oct							
23								
24								
25								
26								
27	7 Oct to 5 Nov							
28								
29								
30								

A ▲

*N.I. Contribution Table letter must be entered overleaf beside the N.I. totals boxes — see the note shown there. This box must be used if the employer wishes to record the N.I. letter while using this side of the sheet.

† If amended cross out previous code

ⓐ If in any week/month the amount in column 4 is more than the amount in column 3, make no entry in column 5.

National Insurance payable	Total carried forward	Total carried forward	Total carried forward
Total carried forward			

P11
(New)

Figure 7.25 Completed form P11
(Reproduced by permission of the Controller of Her Majesty's Stationery Office)

138

5 Subtract the figure in column 4 from the figure in column 3. Enter the amount in column 5. This is then the sum of **money on which the employee owes tax**.

6 Look up the figure in column 5 in the Taxable Pay Tables and this will show the **total tax due to date**. Enter this figure in column 6.

7 The employee will have already paid some of this tax, unless it is week 1 of the tax year, so deduct the previous entry in column 6, tax due to date, from the current entry and this will give the amount of tax due this pay day. If the current entry is less than the previous entry then the employee is refunded the difference.

8 Complete the NI column 1a 'total amount payable by employer and employee' only if the employee earns more than £200 monthly or the lower earnings limit set by the government. Refer to the appropriate NI table and look up the employee's gross pay. This will then show you the **amount of NI** payable. Enter this figure in column 1a.

9 In column 1b enter the figure payable by the employee only.

Step 2

When the tax and NI have been calculated, transfer these figures to the company's payroll (see Figure 7.26), which will give additional space to complete voluntary deductions.

Step 3

Take the figures for tax, NI, voluntary deductions away from the gross pay and complete the figure for net pay (take-home pay).

Step 4

Complete a payslip to be given to the employee from the information on the payroll. This shows the employee how you have arrived at his/her pay.

Step 5

Arrange payment by one of the following means.

1 Credit transfer.

2 Cheque.

3 Cash. Draw up a cash analysis. Withdraw the money from the bank.

PAYROLL

Week or month no.	Date	6 Apr	6 Apr	6 Apr	
Gross pay		246.89			
Gross pay to date		246.89			
Tax free pay		63.25			
Taxable pay to date		183.64			
Tax due to date		45.75			
Tax refund		—			
Deductions	Tax	45.75			
	Nat. Ins.	18.96			
	¹ Superan.	12.05			
	² Social	2.30			
	³ T.U. Sub	4.00			
	4				
	5				
	6				
	Total Deductions	83.06			
Net pay		163.83			
F					
G					
Total amount payable		163.83			
Employer	Nat. Ins	25.76			
	H				
	J				
NAME		Henry Jackson	D. T. Hart	Sally Smith	

The payroll would be completed for all employees.

Figure 7.26 *Payroll*

Follow security procedures (see Section 7, Receiving and making payments). Make up pay packets with exact figure of net pay. When you have made up all the pay packets, the money should correspond exactly with the money withdrawn from the bank on the cash analysis. If **not** check pay packets/ calculations. Employees usually sign to say that they have received their pay and are often asked to check their pay is correct before signing. After this no queries are accepted. Alternatively the money is placed in sealed window pay packets and the notes are folded so that the value of each note is visible. The money can then be checked without breaking the seal. If the seal is broken again no queries are accepted.

> **REMEMBER!** *Confidentiality is essential at all times when dealing with employees' wages and salaries. Do not disclose employees' personal details. Do not disclose employees' gross or net pay. This could lead to much unrest between staff.*

Glossary of wages and salary terms

Gross pay   The total sum of money earned before deductions.

Net pay   Take home pay after all deductions.

NI (National Insurance)   A statutory deduction for anyone over the age of 16 who earns more than the lower earnings limit set by the government. Payment of NI allows the individual to claim benefit if for some reason they are unable to work, ie sickness, unemployment, pregnancy, retirement.

PAYE (Pay As You Earn)   Income tax is paid weekly or monthly, rather than as a lump sum once a year. The amount of income tax paid by an individual depends upon their personal tax code, allocated by the Inland Revenue.

SMP (Statutory Maternity Pay)   Maternity pay can commence 15 weeks before the baby is due (expected week of confinement). There are two rates. The lower rate is paid for up to 18 weeks for any woman who has been in continuous employment with the same organization for 26 weeks before claiming SMP. The higher rate is 90 per cent of the employee's average weekly earning for the first 6 weeks followed by the lower rate for up to 12 weeks. To qualify for the higher rate the woman must have been employed with the same organization for at least 2 years working 16 hours or more each week, or 5 years working 8 hours or more before claiming SMP.

Note:
SMP is eligible for tax and NI, complete P11. The employer can claim back the gross amount of SMP paid from the Inland Revenue by deducting it from the monthly NI contributions.

SSP (Statutory Sick Pay)   All employees aged 16 and over are covered by the statutory sick pay scheme, whenever they are sick for four or more days in a row, provided they pay NI and have been working for the employer for more than eight weeks. SSP is not paid for the first three days of absence: these are called waiting days, but is paid from the fourth day onwards. To calculate, find the average weekly earnings: for weekly paid staff add together their gross earnings on the eight **pay** days before sickness, divide the total by eight. Check with the SSP tables whether the weekly earnings qualify the employee for the standard or lower rate of SSP.

Example   An employee earns £128 per week and is therefore entitled to standard rate SSP £52.50 per week. He is sick Monday through to Friday. There are five qualifying days in the week, but Monday, Tuesday and Wednesday are waiting days so he cannot claim SSP for those three days. Divide the weekly rate by the number of days he has been off sick and multiply by two to calculate his SSP entitlement:

$$£52.50 \div 5 \times 2 = £21$$

Note:
SSP is eligible for tax and NI, complete P11. The maximum payment period is 28 weeks. Depending on the size of the organization the employer can claim back between 80 and 100 per cent of the gross amount of SSP paid from the Inland Revenue by deducting it from the monthly NI contributions (P30). The employee cannot claim SSP if claiming SMP.

Tax forms   The following are frequently used tax forms issued by the Inland Revenue.

P11   Deductions working sheet, completed every pay day. One completed for each employee.

P14   Returned once a year to the Tax Office, showing total figure of pay and tax for each individual employee, plus payments for SSP and SMP.

P15   Employees who have not got a P45, or if it is their first paid job, must complete and send a P15 to the Tax Office, in order to receive a correct Tax Code.

P30   Each month you must complete a P30 payslip and send it with the tax and NI contributions collected that month to the local Tax Office. This must be sent within 14 days of the end of each tax month.

P35   This is an employer's statement of the amount of tax and NI deducted for each employee and the amount of SSP and SMP paid for each employee. The form is returned to the Inspector of Taxes between 5 April and 19 May each year.

P45   When an employee changes jobs during the tax year, the employer issues a P45 that states total earnings to date, tax paid and Tax Code No. Part 1 is sent to the local Tax Office and Parts 2 and 3 are given to the employee to hand to his new employer. The new employer will complete the P11 from the information given and send Part 3 to their local Tax Office.

P46   This has to be completed when a new employee does not produce a P45. It must be signed by the employee and sent to the local Tax Office.

P60   At the end of each tax year each employee receives a P60 that states the total earnings for the year and the amount of tax paid.

IMPORTANT   *All pay records must be kept for at least three years. Calculating wages and salaries and completing all the pay records may seem very complicated to you. The Government issues numerous information leaflets and your local Tax Office is always prepared to give guidance and advice. Make sure you know their address and telephone number. Always take things step by step and seek help if you are not sure.*

COMPUTER APPLICATIONS

Today computers are commonplace in many offices and are used to help the staff perform many administrative tasks.

Figure 8.1 shows the devices that make up a simple computer.

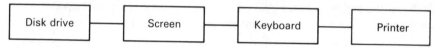

Figure 8.1 *Computer hardware*

Before looking at the applications it is worth while considering two important aspects about computing.

Firstly, the computer, consisting of keyboard, disk drive, screen and printer, is simply a piece of hardware until it is programmed with a software package that gives the instructions to the computer to make it work. This program may be on a floppy disk or installed (stored) on a hard disk. There are numerous software packages on the market and it is beyond the scope of this book to explain in detail how to use any of these packages. We will however briefly look at some software packages that are frequently used in the office.

Secondly, the computer package can only operate with information that has been entered by the operator. Computers do therefore make office tasks easier and quicker but are still dependent on **people** to make them work.

► WORD PROCESSING

Inputting text to the computer via the keyboard, is, in its simplest form , 'typing on computer'. However, the electronic memory of the computer allows the text to be altered on screen and stored on disk to be recalled as and when required. If a word processing package is used a printer is essential, in order to obtain a paper copy of the information stored on disk. There are many different word processing packages available, all of which perform basically the same functions but will require different instructions to make them operate.

Word processing packages are used for producing all types of correspondence. As the text can be amended on screen, the printed copy should be well presented and accurate and this obviously adds to the professional image of the organization. This sort of package is particularly useful for preparing articles and reports, which may need amending. Most word processing packages have a facility to merge a standard letter with a list of addresses, particularly useful for producing personalized circular/form letters.

▶ DATA PROCESSING

This term is used to describe any package that will allow the computer to process and manipulate numbers in addition to text. Two well-known examples are database and spreadsheet. Accounts applications are also popular packages.

Database

This is a means of entering and saving information on computer in a **card index system**, for example, stock records, personnel records, price lists, product information, client information, library book records. The electronic memory of the computer allows the information to be altered and retrieved when required. It is possible for the operator to extract a specific record(s) from the database, eg from a database of personnel records, you could instruct the computer to extract all those employees over the age of 50, provided that their dates of birth had been entered initially. This is obviously much quicker and more accurate than searching through a manual card record system.

Spreadsheet

This program allows the user to perform calculations such as addition, subtraction, multiplication and division simply and quickly on screen. The screen appears as a grid of columns and rows and the data are entered into cells. It is particularly useful for keeping records of petty cash and expenses, together with financial planning. It may be used as a payroll since once the information has been entered the program will perform all calculations. Alternatively, a specific payroll software package may be used. Figure 8.2 overleaf shows a typical spreadsheet screen.

A1:'
Worksheet Range Copy Move File Print Graph Data System Quit
Global Insert Delete Column Erase Titles Window Status Page

	A	B	C	D	E	F	G	H
1								
2								
3								
4								
5								
6								
7								
8								
9								
10								
11								
12								
13								
14								
15								
16								
17								
18								
19								
20								

24-Feb-9*   08:12AM

Figure 8.2 *Spreadsheet screen*

Accounts applications

Various integrated accounts packages are available that will perform the bookkeeping function of an organization on computer. The example shown in Figure 8.3 is a typical screen on an accounts package that shows the range of functions it can perform.

Being an integrated package, if an invoice is produced this will automatically update the sales ledger and decrease the stock records. The package can give you an accurate picture of the organization's financial situation at any time. However, the accuracy of the accounts obviously depends on the accuracy of the entered data.

146

No. of entries :   72

Sales Ledger Postings.   Stock   Control.
Sales Ledger Reports.   Invoice Production.

Purchase Ledger Postings.   Management Reports.
Purchase Ledger Reports.   Utilities Routines.

Nominal Ledger Postings.   Quit.
Nominal Ledger Reports.

Figure 8.3 *Accounts package*

Many other software programs are available depending on the requirements
of the organization, from graphics plotting and design to planning your
journey route. Do not forget that computers are also used for communicating
electronically (see Section 2, Electronic communications).

► SECURITY OF INFORMATION

Security of information held on a computer can be ensured by keeping to the
following rules and procedures.

1   General rules of confidentiality apply.

2   Health and safety procedures should be followed to avoid fire and
    accidents (see Section 1, Health and safety in the office).

3   Security procedures regarding visitors should be adhered to. Visitors
    should not be allowed to wander around the building unsupervised (see
    Section 2, page 44).

4   It is important to keep back-up copies of information contained on disk
    and these should be stored in a fireproof safe. Any floppy disks should be
    locked away when not in use.

5   Information should be saved to disk regularly in case there is a breakdown
    in the computer or a power failure, which could result in information
    being lost.

6   The computer could be programmed to prompt the user for a password
    before it will allow access to the system. Passwords could then be issued to

authorized personnel only. However, in order for passwords to be effective it is important that they are kept confidential.

7 Simple security measures may be adopted, eg

a Ensuring that the information on screen is not visible to other personnel/visitors.

b Closing down the equipment when not in use.

c Taking care with floppy disks to ensure that they are not damaged, or the computer will be unable to read the information they contain.

Data Protection Act

Following the introduction of the Data Protection Act in 1984, organizations who hold information (data) on computer, which could identify individuals ie personal details, must register with the data protection registrar. The registrar will approve the purpose for which data about people is being put on to computer. The organization must then ensure that the information is used only for the purpose specified. The Act also gives employees, customers and members of the public the right to inspect any information kept on computer about themselves.

This act only applies to information contained on computer and not data processed by manual methods.

Registration forms can be obtained from main post offices or from the Office of the Data Protection Registrar, Springfield House, Water Lane, Wilmslow, Cheshire.

> **IMPORTANT** Copyright law: do remember that software programs are copyright and it is illegal to copy a program without permission. However, some producers do give permission in their instruction manual for a back-up copy **only** to be made.

REPROGRAPHICS

Reprographics means producing copies of an original document. All organizations however small or large require copies of documents. It is highly probable that you have taken copies of documents yourself and possibly visited your local library to take a photocopy. This could be for any of the following reasons.

- The original document has to be sent away and we wish to retain a copy.
- We wish to retain the original document and send a copy.
- Unless we keep copies of correspondence we cannot remember what action has been taken.
- A copy provides proof of actions taken or proposed.
- We require a copy purely for information.

▶ REPROGRAPHICS EQUIPMENT

There are various ways we can take a copy of a document. These methods are illustrated in Table 9.1. It is important, however, that you consider the following points before deciding on which method to use.

1   The type of document to be copied, eg single sheet, multiple page, bound document, coloured original, size of document.

2   Quality of copy required.

3   Number of copies required.

4   Cost.

Most offices have access to, or are equipped with, one or more photocopiers. Various types are available and the choice depends on requirements.

Photocopiers

Table 9.2 is a simple chart to compare the features and functions to be found on a typical standard desktop photocopier with those of a more advanced free-standing model. There are many models to choose from and many

Table 9.1 Methods of reproducing documents

Method	Advantages	Disadvantages	Materials required
Photocopying	Gives an exact copy of high quality. Quick, clean and easy to use. Can create documents by cutting and rearranging articles and recopying. Many additional features: see Table 9.2	Single sheet feed copiers are expensive and time-consuming for large numbers of copies. Equipment can break down. Equipment can be expensive to purchase or hire. Colour is expensive.	Copier paper Toner Anti-static cleaning material
Carbon copy	Convenient. Copy can be made at the same time as the original is being written or typed. Produces an exact copy of the original. Will only copy typewritten or handwritten work. Very cheap. No equipment required.	Copy not as clear and professional looking. After more than two copies blurring will occur.	Carbon paper Copier paper Correction material
Fax copy	Convenient if fax machine in office. Produces an exact copy.	Only suitable for single copies. Expensive as require thermal copy paper. Copy will fade over a period of time.	Thermal copy paper
Computer printer	Multiple original copies can be produced.	Can only produce copies of documents already entered on disk. Rather slow in comparison to photocopier.	Paper: single sheet or continuous stationery. Ink cartridge
Spirit duplicating	Ideal for multiple copies of handwritten/typewritten docu-	Not professional. An exact copy of an original can only be produced by	Spirit Spirit masters and carbons

	...ments to be used internally. Up to 100 copies from one master (possibly 200 depending on quality required). Different colours can be achieved with different coloured carbons. Cheap.	...preparing a thermal master first. Carbon can be messy. Care must be taken when storing spirit.	Copying paper Cleaning material
Ink duplicating	Excellent for long runs of documents from 50 to 1000. Stencils once made may be stored and used again. Can produce different coloured copies by using different coloured ink drums. Ink duplicators are now being updated to combine the convenience of photocopying with the lower cost of ink duplicating on long runs. These machines will automatically cut the stencil, run off the copies required and discard the stencil for you.	An exact copy of an original can only be produced by preparing a thermal master first. Otherwise stencils are best cut on the typewriter or using an electronic stencil cutter. Can be messy.	Ink Ink stencil Duplicating copier paper (absorbent) Cleaning material
Off-set litho duplicating	Nearest to commercial printing. Can produce large numbers of copies from one plate, eg 5000 copies from a paper plate.	Training required. A paper or metal plate of the original must be produced.	Plates Ink Copier paper Cleaning material

manufacturers, eg Canon, Minolta, Rank Xerox, Kodak, Sharp, to name only a few. From the large range available an organization can decide which model will meet its own particular requirements.

Table 9.2 Photocopiers		
	Desktop	**Advanced: free standing**
Dimensions	Width 538 mm	Width 890 mm
	Height 271 mm	Height 1185 mm
	Depth 598 mm	Depth 685 mm
Weight	Approx. 17 kg	Approx. 180 kg
Speed	15 copies per minute	60 copies per minute
Storage capacity of paper cassette	250 sheets	3000 sheets
Features	One original copied at a time	As for standard model plus automatic copies 1–999
	Adjust toner density	Help message display that gives instructions
	Automatic copies 1–99	
	Will diagnose faults automatically and alert the operator	Will reduce documents
		Will enlarge documents
	Manual feed by-pass for double-sided copies	Automatic double-sided copying
		Frame and punch hole erase
		Automatic collating
		Automatic stapling
		Security access codes
		Automatic feed through of original documents to be copied
Colour	No	No

Note:
Colour copiers are now available. Some copiers will accept two or three different colours of toner and therefore give impressive copies in for example: blue, red and black. Full colour copiers will reproduce colour photographs and pictures but are presently very expensive in comparison to standard black and white photocopiers.

Small organizations or organizations that do not require many copies may choose to use an outside agency's photocopier. Many companies now offer photocopying services. Other organizations will have their own reprographic equipment that individuals use as and when required. Organizations that produce a lot of documents may have their own reprographics department with trained staff and specialist equipment. To have one photocopier, rather than several around the building, means that the organization can choose to have one highly sophisticated machine rather than several standard models. However, because photocopying is so popular these days, some organizations with a reprographics department will still have small photocopiers around the building for convenience.

▶ WORKING IN THE REPROGRAPHICS DEPARTMENT

You will need to know how to use the equipment and most suppliers of equipment will provide training. If training is not arranged, refer to instruction booklets and seek help from your supervisor or the supplier as necessary. The work can be technical and this is why many reprographics clerks are referred to as technicians. A good reprographics clerk will be conscientious and take a pride in their work, so that the quality of the copies produced is to a high standard. They must also be reliable and able to meet deadlines following instructions given.

Any work for the reprographics department is usually accompanied by a requisition form (Figure 9.1), which gives details of the work to be done.

COPYING/PRINTING REQUISITION FORM

Name: .... Date:..

Dept: .... Time: ....

No. of copies required ....

Date required........................... (Unless special arrangements are

made allow at least 24 hours)

Instructions

....

....

....

....

Figure 9.1 *Copying/printing requisition form*

In addition to the reprographics equipment, the following items of equipment are frequently required in the department.

1 Long-arm, heavy-duty stapler.

2 Guillotine.

3 Binding machine

   a Punching and binding machine (Figure 9.2). Pull the handle to punch holes and release the handle to insert plastic comb binding.

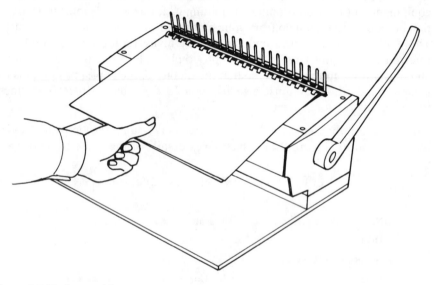

Figure 9.2 *Binding machine*

   b Thermal binding machines. Using heat and PVC covers, up to 200 sheets can be bound in 30 seconds. Not as easy to add/remove pages as with comb binding.

4 Collator. An electric machine that will help with sorting duplicated reports and multi-page documents into sets. This is much quicker than sorting by hand.

5 Shredder. Unwanted documents/paper may be shredded. The paper may then be used by some organizations as packing material. Also essential for destroying confidential documents.

6 Computer and laser printer. Many reprographics departments now have a computer with desktop publishing package for designing leaflets, stationery, etc, without having to send it to an outside printing company. A special printer is required so that pictures and graphics can be produced.

Tips on copying material

- When photocopying, clean the glass regularly. Ensure that the paper you use is uncreased and untorn to prevent paper jams. Check the toner: lack of toner makes copies very faint. Most machines will alert you when more toner is required.
- Check you have good materials. Check your carbon paper is not too worn or creased as a crease will produce a 'tree effect' on your copy. Stencils should be well cut and prepared if you expect to get a good copy from them. Use the correct quality copier paper.
- Check the quality of the original. A poor original will obviously produce a poor copy.
- Save money by reducing the number of copies taken. Can the article be reduced to A5 from A4? Take double-sided copies to save paper. Cut and paste articles; if part of the article is not required or the original contains a lot of wasted space. Don't copy more than requested. Many technicians tend to copy a few more 'for good measure'.
- Ensure that the equipment is cleaned and maintained regularly.

Law and security

Copyright law

If you are working in the reprographics department it is important that you remember copyright law, but it is generally felt 'fair' to copy for personal use and not for resale **one** copy of printed materials provided it does not amount to more than one complete chapter of a book or 10 per cent of a short book, report or article. Illustrations may not be copied by themselves, only if they form part of a copied extract.

> **IMPORTANT** Copyright law gives legal protection to authors and writers of music, plays, computer programs, etc so that work cannot be copied. If work is copyright it will tell you so and you will usually see the symbol ©. Copyright lasts for 50 years after the author's death or 25 years after the edition was first published.

Educational establishments can obtain a licence from the Copyright Licensing Agency to make multiple class copies from books.

The following addresses may be useful:

The British Copyright Council, 29–33 Berners Street, London W1P 4AA
The Copyright Licensing Agency, 90 Tottenham Court Road, London W1P 9HE

Security of information

1 General rules of confidentiality and security of visitors apply.

2 Do not leave original documents and copies unattended and on view.

3 Return confidential documents in sealed envelopes.

4 Return important documents **by hand** if practical.

5 In some organizations only authorized personnel have access to the reprographics room and the photocopier can only be used by those issued with a security key, code or card. This is also a way of keeping costs down.

MAKING ARRANGEMENTS

Most organizations need to make arrangements to meet people. Customers and clients will be visited by representatives from your organization, and sales representatives may wish to visit you. There are trade fairs, exhibitions and conferences all over the world that staff from your organization may wish to attend. You may work for an organization that has branches throughout the country or throughout the world and staff may travel to them.

If you work in an office it is therefore important that you know how to make travel arrangements and organize meetings, both of which will involve all your **communication and administrative skills**.

► ARRANGING TRAVEL

Procedures and requirements

Organizations may have various procedures for making travel arrangements, some of which are as follows.

1 They may use an outside travel agency, preferably one that specializes in business travel.

2 They may have their own internal travel bureaux with trained staff. This is particularly common in large multinational organizations where staff are constantly travelling abroad. The company will then have its own account with airlines and hotel groups.

3 One person may be allocated the responsibility of organizing travel. This means that the person will become highly knowledgeable of the travel industry and will be able to build up good relationships with travel agents, hotels, airlines, car hire companies, etc. It also means that all reference materials required, for example timetables, hotel guides, maps, can be centralized.

4 Individuals may be responsible for arranging their own travel or their 'boss's' travel. This is usual in small organizations and organizations that do not undertake many business trips.

157

Let us look at the situation where you are responsible for organizing the travel arrangements for Mr Roberts, the company sales manager. What would you have to do? The first thing is to find out his requirements by asking questions and writing the answers down.

Question 1: *Where is he travelling to?*
One destination or more? In the UK or abroad?

Question 2: *When? What are his dates of departure and return?*
On what date does he plan to start the journey? How long will the visit last? How long will he stay in each place? What will be the date of return?

Question 3: *What form of transport is to be used?*
Is the travel by road, rail, air, sea (not common in business, unless it is necessary to take a vehicle with equipment and materials for display/sales purposes abroad) or perhaps a combination of two, eg air/road, air/rail. Is first class travel required or will economy class be satisfactory?

Question 4: *Will accommodation be required?*
If so what type: five star or one star rated (five star being the most superior accommodation)? Is a private suite required to meet customers/clients? Single or double room: is your manager taking his partner? Has Mr Roberts any preferences regarding hotel/location?

Question 5: *What will happen in his absence?*
Have arrangements been made for covering his duties or not? Will appointments need to be cancelled?

Question 6: *What is the purpose of the visit?*
Do appointments need to be made? Does an itinerary need to be prepared?

Once you have gathered all the information, then you can start to make arrangements. These arrangements will vary depending on the destination of the trip. The details that follow will show you the arrangements that need to be considered whether you are making national or international travel arrangements.

National and international travel

Book travel tickets

1   Check with timetables for the most appropriate departure and arrival times. Remember that the airport, ferry port, railway station may be a good distance from the hotel or meeting place and therefore allow for

(a)

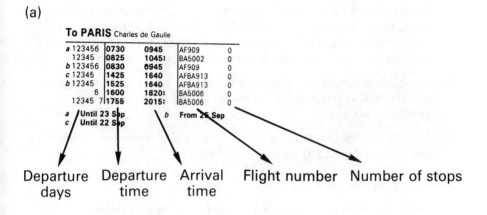

1 = Monday
2 = Tuesday
3 = Wednesday
4 = Thursday
5 = Friday
6 = Saturday
7 = Sunday

(b)

From PARIS Charles de Gaulle

12345	0730‡	0745	BA5001	0
12345	1130‡	1145	BA5003	0
a 12345	1330	1350	AFBA912	0
b 12345	1330	1450	AFBA912	0
6	1905‡	1920	BA5007	0
a 12345 7	2055	2115	AF916	0
c 12345 7	2055	2215	AF916	0
5	2100‡	2115	BA5009	0

a Until 22 Sep   b From 25 Sep
c From 24 Sep

Figure 10.1 *Timetable: (a) Manchester to Paris, (b) Paris to Manchester*

travelling time. Also remember the time difference across the world.
Figure 10.1 is an example of an airline timetable. You will see that the
return journey from Paris to Manchester appears to take much less time.
This is because of the time difference between Manchester and Paris (see
Reference guide 4).

2 Air tickets may be purchased direct from the airline company or the travel agent. Rail tickets may be purchased from British Rail booking offices or travel agents who are authorized British Rail booking offices. Ferry tickets may be purchased from ferry companies or travel agents.

3 Give precise details of the type of ticket you require and the departure/arrival times. If you have any problems the travel agent or company will be able to advise you.

4 Arrange for the tickets to be sent to you or if it is a late booking to be collected on departure.

Book hotel accommodation

1 Find a convenient hotel either close to the airport/station or to the meeting place. The following will help you:

a National and international hotel guides produced by large hotel groups; accommodation guides produced by motoring organizations and tourist boards.

b Yellow Pages for national travel.

c Your travel agent, who will be able to refer to the ABC Corporate Services Worldwide Hotel Guide.

2 Make a reservation by:

a Contacting the hotel direct or the central reservations booking office of large hotel groups. These booking offices will be based in the UK and they will check the availability of one of their hotels anywhere in the world and book it for you. This avoids language and currency problems.

b Consulting your travel agent who will book the accommodation for you.

c Confirming your reservation with the hotel in writing, either by letter (see Figure 10.2), fax or Telex and ask for confirmation of the booking to be returned to you. If you are booking through a travel agent, then ensure that you receive written confirmation of the booking from them.

Check documents required

1 Is a passport required and if so is your sales manager's passport current?

2 Does the country to be visited require a visa? Some countries require a visa in addition to a passport. A visa means that the reason for the trip has been approved by the country and permission to visit granted. In general British subjects travelling within the EC do not require a visa. For

```
Our Ref: JR/sk


5th March 199*


The Reservations Dept
The Post Hall Hotel
KENSINGTON
London
WC1 2BN


Dear Sirs

I am writing to confirm my telephone reservation with you for a single room
with private facilities for Monday 25th and Tuesday 26th March 199*.  Please
note that on Tuesday 26th March I shall require breakfast at 0600 hours,
which I understand is acceptable to you.

I should be grateful if you could send me a map of your location with
confirmation of this booking.

Yours faithfully




J ROBERTS
Sales Manager
```

Figure 10.2 *Letter of confirmation*

countries outside the EC consult your travel agent or the consulate of the
country to be visited (see Reference guide 3).

3 Prepare an itinerary giving, in particular, departure and arrival times,
   accommodation arrangements, details of meetings, social events. See
   example: Figure 10.3.

Arrange finance for international travel

Check with your sales manager which of the following will be required.

1 Foreign currency. This is available from travel agents, banks, bureaux de
   change at airports. Currency is useful for small payments, such as taxi
   fares, tips, refreshments.

2 Traveller's cheques. This is the safest means of carrying money abroad.

ITINERARY

MR ROBERTS

Monday 25 March to Wednesday 27 March 199*

MONDAY 25 MARCH   Depart 0823 hours Manchester Piccadilly Railway Station
Arrive 1057 hours London Euston

1200 hours Lunch London, Strand Road Branch
Mr Hamilton-Smith, Branch Manager

1930 hours Dinner (formal dress)
Institute of Marketing
Garden Hotel, Knightsbridge

(HOTEL: THE POST HALL HOTEL, KENSINGTON, WC1 2BN. TEL: 071-246 7824)

TUESDAY 26 MARCH   Depart 0725 hours London Heathrow Flight KL112
Amsterdam
Arrive 0930 hours Amsterdam

1030 Meeting with Mr Hans,
Karl Dole & Co Ltd, Herengracht 233,
1016 DG Amsterdam

1300 hours Lunch with Mr Kalver
Caransa Hotel, Rembrandtsplein 19, 1017 CT Amsterdam

Depart 1700 hours Amsterdam, Flight KL125 London
Heathrow
Arrive 1710 hours London Heathrow

(HOTEL: THE POST HALL HOTEL AS ABOVE)

WEDNESDAY 27 MARCH   Depart 1000 hours London Euston Railway Station
Arrive 1237 hours Manchester Piccadilly

Figure 10.3 *Itinerary for trip to Amsterdam via London*

3 International charge card.

4 International credit card.

5 UK cheque book and Eurocheque card.

Use the following checklist to make sure you have all the documents required for the trip.

.... Tickets

.... Confirmation of hotel reservation

.... Itinerary

.... Correspondence relating to purpose of visit

.... Car hire details if required

.... Driving licence

.... Passport if required

.... Visa if required

.... Vaccination certificates if required

.... Insurance cover certificate if required

.... E111 if travelling to EC country

.... Finance

Arrange a hire car

If your sales manager is not using his or her own transport then check to see if a hire car is required on arriving at the airport/railway station, either in this country or abroad.

1   Look in your Yellow Pages or local directory under car hire. This will give local, national and international car hire companies with central reservation booking office telephone numbers. By phoning them locally they will arrange for a car to be delivered to any destination required in this country or abroad. Again this avoids language and currency problems.

2   Enquire whether an international driving licence is required.

Medical cover and insurance

1   Are any vaccinations required for the countries to be visited? Check with Table 10.1, which lists diseases and vaccination recommendations.

2   If travelling within the EC obtain an E111 form from your local post office: once completed, this allows free emergency medical treatment in EC countries.

Table 10.1 Diseases, precautions and recommendations

	Disease risk areas	How caught	Vaccination	Vaccination certificate needed?
HIV/AIDS	World-wide.	From having sex with an infected person; by infected blood entering your body either by contaminated needles or syringes or by transfusion with infected blood or inadequately sterilized equipment; from infected mother to baby.	None available.	No, but some countries have introduced HIV antibody testing for some visitors (or require an HIV antibody test certificate for some visitors. See note below).
Cholera	Africa, Asia, Middle East and South America, especially in conditions of poor hygiene and sanitation.	From contaminated food or water.	Usually 2 injections by your doctor.	Some countries may require evidence of vaccination. Certificate valid for 6 months.
Viral Hepatitis A	Most parts of the world but especially in conditions of poor hygiene and sanitation.	From contaminated food or water.	Immunoglobulin if not already immune.	No.
Viral Hepatitis B	World-wide.	By intimate and sexual contact with an infected person; from injections with infected blood or needles (as AIDS).	Your doctor will advise on the need for vaccination.	No.
Malaria	Africa, Asia, Central and South America.	Bite from infected mosquito.	None, but anti-malarial tablets are available.	No.

Poliomyelitis	Everywhere except Australia, New Zealand, Europe and North America.	Direct contact with an infected person; rarely by contaminated water or food.	Drops by mouth in 3 doses (spacing depends upon age). Reinforcing dose advised after 10 years.	No.
Rabies	Many parts of the world.	Bite or scratch from an infected animal.	Vaccination may be advised after a bite. Get advice from a doctor immediately.	No.
Tetanus	World-wide but particularly dangerous in places where medical facilities not readily available.	Any skin-penetrating wound, especially if soiled.	Vaccination is safe, effective and gives long-lasting protection.	No.
Tuberculosis	Asia, Africa, Central and South America.	Airborne from infectious person, and from drinking unpasteurized milk.	Skin test and injection at least 2 months before travel.	No.
Typhoid	Everywhere except Australia, New Zealand, Europe, North America, in conditions of poor hygiene and sanitation.	Contaminated food, water or milk.	2 injections from your doctor, 4–6 weeks apart. Revaccination by 1 injection usually after 3 years.	No.
Yellow Fever	Africa and South America.	Bite from infected mosquito.	1 injection at a yellow fever vaccination centre at least 10 days before you go abroad.	Yes. Certificate valid for 10 years.

Smallpox has been eradicated world-wide and there is NO requirement for the vaccination of travellers.
Note: If in doubt about HIV antibody test certificate requirements check the current position with the Embassy or High Commission in London of the country concerned.

3 Obtain insurance cover for personal accident, loss of property, travel delay/cancellation and motor insurance if appropriate. If travelling outside the EC ensure you have medical cover. Travel insurance is available from travel agents, banks and insurance companies.

> **IMPORTANT** Do consult your sales manager if you have any problems with the above. It may be that you can agree alternative arrangements.

► ARRANGING MEETINGS

From a very early age we all arrange to meet people. This is so that we can **talk, discuss matters** and **make decisions**. Business meetings are held for exactly the same reasons. Some business meetings are **informal** and others **formal**, depending, for example, on the nature of meeting, the subject(s) under discussion, the people involved.

Informal meetings

A manager may call his or her team together to discuss a new company policy. A meeting may be called regarding a staff outing or social event. A trade union representative may call a meeting of members to discuss changes in wages/salary structure. These are examples of informal meetings, but even informal meetings require organization.

Date and time

A date and time must be arranged. This may be decided by one person, in the hope that as many people as possible will be able to attend, or each person invited to the meeting may be consulted individually to find a convenient date and time. This is very time-consuming and if there are more than five or six participants it becomes very difficult to arrange. Contact with the participants is usually made by telephone, fax, Telex or electronic mail if a speedy response is required. It is particularly helpful if electronic mail is available with access to each user's diary. This means that the user's diary is kept on computer so that you can see when the person is available and automatically update their diary from your own computer terminal.

Accommodation/venue

Suitable accommodation will be required. The size of the room should match the number of people attending: for example, for a big meeting the room must be large enough to cope with the numbers invited. The meeting may be held in the manager's own office, a committee room or the company canteen may be used for a trade union or staff meeting. Perhaps an outside venue will be required. Hotels will provide meeting rooms for small numbers, eg two to six people right up to large meetings/conferences of 150 people or more, depending on their facilities. Many other organizations are now offering rooms for meetings, eg colleges, professional centres, social clubs.

Notifying

This can be done in several ways. If the meeting is urgent then a telephone call will have to suffice. If all the participants are based within an organization, then notices may be posted around the building. Alternatively people may be invited personally by letter or memorandum, giving notice of the meeting and stating the time, date and place. It may also be necessary to enclose a map giving directions to the venue. Do remember that fax and electronic mail can help to speed up this communication process.

Equipment/materials

Special equipment may be required. For example, a sales manager may wish to give a presentation to his or her team of a new product to be launched and may require items such as a flip chart, overhead projector to show acetate transparencies, a slide projector and a screen to show slides, video equipment to show a video. If these items of equipment are available within your organization, they will usually need to be booked in advance of the meeting; if not, they may need to be hired from an outside agency.

Refreshments

Requirements will vary from, say, coffee/tea to coffee/tea/lunch, depending on the time of day and length of the meeting. For example, if lunch is required determine what type of lunch, at what time and for how many. Again it may be that there are facilities within your organization for catering and arrangements can be made with the catering manager. If not an outside caterer will need to be arranged and three or four should be approached to compare and obtain the best services and prices.

Some meetings have to be held by law, eg the Annual General Meeting (AGM) of a Public Limited Company. If you are a member of a building society then you will be invited to attend their AGM every year, so that members can consider the financial position of the company. Other meetings not required by law, but essential for decisions to be made regarding the organization, are those such as council meetings, health authority meetings, board meetings (meetings of the directors of a company), health and committee meetings. These will be conducted in a formal fashion and involve more paper work than informal meetings to ensure that all participants are kept informed about what is happening.

To inform people a **notice** of the meeting is sent to all participants by the secretary. Fourteen days notice of the meeting is usually required or 21 days for an AGM. An example of a formal notice is given in Figure 10.4.

The notice is often combined with the agenda. The **agenda** gives details of the matters to be dealt with and the order in which they will occur during the

---

SHEPPERTON INDUSTRIES PLC
APPELTON INDUSTRIAL ESTATE
APPELTON
WA3 2BP

30 March 199*

NOTICE OF BOARD MEETING

Notice is hereby given that a meeting of the directors will be held at The Dalton Hotel, Appelton on 24 April 199* at 1000 hours, at which your presence is requested.

....
Secretary

Figure 10.4 *Example of formal notice*

meeting. Though these matters will vary depending on the type of meeting, most formal meetings adopt the following pattern.

- Apologies for absence will be read out.
- Minutes of the last meeting will be read.
- Discussion will follow on matters arising from the minutes.
- Correspondence received will be dealt with.
- Special matters relating to the meeting or new items will be discussed.
- Any other business will follow so that members can raise any additional items not covered by the agenda.
- The date and time of the next meeting will be fixed.

An example of a notice of a meeting together with an agenda is given in Figure 10.5.

Note:
A copy of the minutes of the last meeting, together with copies of any reports or documents that need careful consideration by the members are often enclosed with the notice and agenda. Do check with the secretary/ chairperson about this.

During the course of the meeting, the secretary will take notes of the proceedings and these notes will form the official record of what has happened, known as the **minutes of the meeting**. There are various ways to write the minutes, but they are usually drawn up following a standardized layout that uses the same headings as the agenda. See example of minutes, Figure 10.6.

Minutes outline what has happened in the meeting and the action(s) to be taken. In particular they record all decisions made. At a formal meeting decisions are reached in the following way.

1 The **motion** (item to be put forward for consideration) is put to the meeting by a member who proposes it.

2 This motion is then seconded by a member who supports the motion.

3 If a member feels that an alteration to the wording of the proposal is required, this is called an **amendment**.

4 The chairperson will then present the motion to the members in its final form.

5 The members will vote on the motion with a show of hands.

6 If the vote is for the motion then the motion is passed/carried and it becomes a **resolution**.

```
┌─────────────────────────────────────────────────────────┐
│                                                           │
│                 SHEPPERTON INDUSTRIES PLC                 │
│               APPELTON INDUSTRIAL ESTATE                  │
│                      APPELTON                             │
│                      WA3 2BP                              │
│                                                           │
│   30 March 199*                                           │
│                                                           │
│   HEALTH AND SAFETY COMMITTEE MEETING                     │
│                                                           │
│   There will be a meeting of the above committee on       │
│   18th April 199* at 1400 hours, in Committee Room A.     │
│                                                           │
│                        AGENDA                             │
│                                                           │
│   1.  Apologies for absence                               │
│   2.  Minutes of the last meeting                         │
│   3.  Matters arising from the minutes                    │
│   4.  Correspondence                                      │
│   5.  First-aid boxes                                     │
│   6.  Report on emergency evacuation procedure            │
│   7.  Any other business                                  │
│   8.  Date and time of next meeting                       │
│                                                           │
│                                                           │
│   ........................                                │
│   Secretary                                               │
│                                                           │
└─────────────────────────────────────────────────────────┘
```

Figure 10.5 *Example of a notice of a meeting and an agenda*

Conduct of formal meetings

So that the meeting is conducted in an orderly fashion and the items for discussion are all dealt with fairly it is necessary for someone to have authority and control over the meeting. This person is the **chairperson**. The chairperson is appointed by the **members** (that is the people allowed to attend and participate in the meeting). The chairperson will also prepare the agenda in consultation with the secretary, check a draft copy of the minutes and sign them as a correct record. At a formal meeting any items to be raised are usually addressed through the chair, eg 'Mr Chairman/Madam Chairman, I

170

SHEPPERTON INDUSTRIES PLC

MINUTES OF MEETING

A meeting of the Health and Safety Committee was held in comittee room A at the Head office of Shepperton Industries PLC on 18th April 199* at 1400 hours.

PRESENT

Mr B. Thompson (Chairman)
Mr J. Hunt
Mrs E. Kophamel
Miss C. Whaley
Miss B. Wragg
Mrs B. Dawson (Secretary)

1: APOLOGIES FOR ABSENCE
The Secretary reported that Mr H Jackson was unable to attend as he was on holiday.

2: MINUTES OF THE LAST MEETING
The minutes of the last meeting, held on 10th February 199* were read, approved and signed by the chairman.

3. MATTERS ARISING FROM THE MINUTES
The secretary reported that the obstruction on the administration corridor had now been cleared.

4. CORRESPONDENCE
The secretary read an invitation from the Health and Safety Executive for a representative from the company to attend an Accident Prevention Seminar on 6th June 199*.

It was proposed by Miss C. Whaley that Mrs E. Kophamel be our delegate; this was seconded by Mr Hunt and carried unanimously.

5. FIRST-AID BOXES
Miss B. Wragg expressed concern about the theft of first-aid boxes from public areas. The chairman agreed to review this situation and see what could be done to improve security.

6. REPORT ON EMERGENCY EVACUATION PROCEDURE
Miss Whaley reported that the time taken to evacuate the building at the last fire drill on the 5th March had been 4 minutes 20 seconds and all staff appeared to follow the correct procedure. This was felt by the committee to be acceptable and it was agreed that a copy of this report should be placed on the staff notice-board. Mrs Dawson agreed to arrange this.

7. ANY OTHER BUSINESS
There was no other business.

8. DATE AND TIME OF NEXT MEETING
The date of the next meeting was fixed for 15th June, 199* at 1400 hours.

The chairman declared the meeting closed at 1540 hours.

SIGNED .... DATE ....

    B. Thompson
    (Chairman)

Figure 10.6 *Example of minutes of a meeting*

would like to . . . . ' The chairperson also holds a **casting vote** if there is an equal number of votes for and against a motion; in other words the chairperson will have a second vote to make the final decision.

The chairperson is assisted by the **secretary** who ensures that all the paper work is in order and all arrangements for the meeting have been made, even though the secretary may delegate these tasks to someone else.

On the day of the meeting the secretary should check that:

1 The room and layout of furniture are correct.

2 Reception have been informed of the meeting and which members to expect.

3 Refreshments are in hand.

4 Spare copies of the agenda and minutes are available for members.

5 All documents are available for the meeting, eg correspondence received and apologies for absence.

6 Check that the attendance register is signed by all members present at the meeting.

REMEMBER! *All items discussed and decisions made in a meeting are highly confidential and any information obtained from agendas/minutes should be treated as such. The only exception is a public meeting, but discretion must still be used about disclosing information. Agendas and minutes should be circulated in sealed envelopes marked 'private and confidential' and only issued to members of the meeting, unless you are instructed otherwise by the chairperson or secretary. Copies of all documentation should be kept in locked cabinets.*

Business Administration

DIARY PAGES

Keep this diary to build up a picture of your experiences in business administration. This will provide evidence for your assessor when you are ready to claim competence for a unit and also help you to complete your competence transcript. The unit numbers given on each page will help you to relate the activity you have undertaken to the appropriate unit. Space has been left on each page for you to indicate whether the activity was undertaken on the job, that is in the work place, or off the job, while in a training environment.

At the end of your experiences ask for verification that the information you have given is correct by asking your turors/supervisors to complete the details below. Then sign it yourself to say that you have completed the information as accurately as possible.

Verified by:

Name	Position/Organization	Signature	Comments

The information contained in this diary has been completed as accurately as possible.

Candidate's signature ....

PERSONAL MEMORANDA

Name ....
Home address ....

....

Centre name ....
Centre no. ....
Centre tel. no. ....
Candidate no. ....
Course coordinator ....

Useful telephone numbers

Local international airport ....
Local railway station ....
Local general hospital ....
Local post office ....
Local travel agent ....
Directory enquiries ....
Fire, police, ambulance, cave rescue, coastguard,
   mountain rescue ....
Other frequently used telephone numbers:

....
....
....
....
....

Work placement undertaken at

....

From .... To ....
Tasks undertaken ....

....
....

From .... To ....
Tasks undertaken ....

....
....

From .... To ....
Tasks undertaken ....

....
....

UNIT ....

Date	Document drafted (Letter, memorandum, report, table of figures, etc)	Purpose of document	State whether 'real' work or paper-based assignment	On/off the job

Business communications (written)

Diary page

175

UNIT ....

Date	Equipment used	Message received from	Message sent to	On/off the job

Electronic communications

Diary page

UNIT ....

Date	Software package used	Indicate what you used the package for	On/off the job

Diary page

Computer applications

UNIT ....

Date	Documents filed	Classification system	Filing equipment	Action taken	On/off the job

Diary page

Filing documents

UNIT ....

Date	Documents extracted Information abstracted	Where from	Action taken	On/off the job

Diary page   Obtaining documents/information

179

UNIT ....

Date	Money deposited at bank: give details	Money withdrawn from bank: give details	Payments received: give details	Payments made: give details	On/off the job

Diary page

Financial record keeping/handling cash

180

UNIT .... (Petty cash records must be kept for a minimum of one month)

Date	Item purchased	Amount	Action taken (indicate if petty cash voucher completed. Did you complete the petty cash book?)	On/off the job

Diary page

Financial record keeping/petty cash

UNIT ....

Date	Details of document checked	Action taken (indicate passed for payment, or how errors have been dealt with)	On/off the job

Documents checked for payment (invoices and expense claim forms)

Diary page

UNIT ....

Date	Instruction on organization's health and safety policy received: give details	Equipment faults reported: give details	Accidents reported: give details	On/off the job

Diary page

Health and safety

183

UNIT .... (It is recommended that a minimum of 30 items should be handled in total)

Date	Mail received	Action taken (state whether distributed to departments, placed in staff pigeon holes, suspicious packages reported)	On/off the job

Handling incoming/internal mail

Diary page

184

UNIT .... (It is recommended that a minimum of 30 items should be handled in total)

Date	Mail for despatch	Action taken (state whether weighed, stamps affixed, franked, postage book completed, item taken to post office)	On/off the job

Diary page

Handling outgoing/internal mail

UNIT ....

Date	Purpose of meeting	No. of participants	Action taken	State if 'real' meeting or paper-based assignment	On/off the job

Diary page

Arranging meetings

186

UNIT ....

Date	Time	Message received from (indicate if message was transcribed from answering machine)	Action taken (who was the message passed to, was the message verbal or written, how did you handle urgent messages?)	On/off the job

Receive and relay oral and written messages

Diary page

187

UNIT .... (It is recommended that a minimum of 30 callers should be received in total, in order to claim competence)

Date	Caller's name	Purpose of visit	Action taken	On/off the job

Diary page   Receiving visitors

UNIT ....

Date	Reception area maintained at (name of organization)	Action taken

Diary page

Maintaining a reception area

189

UNIT ....

Date	Arrangements made	State if 'real' work or paper-based assignment	On/off the job

Diary page

Making travel arrangements

UNIT ....

Date	Documents prepared	Manual or computerized system	State if 'real' work or paper-based assignment	On/off the job

Ordering and supplying goods and services

Diary page

191

UNIT .... (It is recommended that to gain competence you should carry out this job for at least a one-month period)

Date	No. of copies produced	Equipment used	Special features (eg double-sided, reduced, collated, cut and paste)	On/off the job

Diary page

Reprographics

UNIT ....

Date	Stock items issued	To	Action taken (records updated: indicate if manual or computerized, new stock requested/ordered)	On/off the job

Diary page

Stock handling

193

UNIT ....

Date	Caller	Action taken (required information given, message taken, call transferred)	Equipment used	On/off the job

Diary page

Dealing with incoming telephone calls

194

UNIT .... (A minimum of 30 calls must be made to claim competence)

Date	Time	Tel no. including code	Action taken (information requested, message given, caller connected)	Equipment used	On/off the job

Diary page   Dealing with outgoing telephone calls

195

UNIT ....

Date	

Additional diary page for personal use

196

REFERENCE GUIDES

R1 *Outline map of Great Britain*

London

	London	Aberdeen	Birmingham	Bristol	Cardiff	Carlisle	Dover	Edinburgh	Exeter	Fort William	Glasgow	Holyhead	Inverness	Leeds	Liverpool	Manchester	Newcastle	Norwich	Nottingham
Aberdeen	543																		
Birmingham	118	430																	
Bristol	119	511	85																
Cardiff	155	533	107	45															
Carlisle	307	234	197	275	297														
Dover	77	630	203	203	238	393													
Edinburgh	405	130	293	373	395	98	460												
Exeter	200	584	157	81	120	347	246	455											
Fort William	523	159	402	484	505	209	599	135	556										
Glasgow	405	149	291	372	393	97	490	45	444	103									
Holyhead	267	457	155	232	209	223	351	327	305	433	321								
Inverness	569	105	453	537	558	260	656	158	610	66	171	488							
Leeds	196	336	115	216	236	122	268	205	288	331	215	165	382						
Liverpool	210	361	98	178	200	125	295	222	250	334	220	106	377	72					
Manchester	197	354	88	167	188	118	283	218	239	325	214	125	379	43	34				
Newcastle	278	239	198	291	311	58	348	107	372	243	150	262	268	91	170	141			
Norwich	115	501	161	243	278	284	169	365	323	492	379	298	548	173	242	183	258		
Nottingham	128	414	59	151	170	186	211	268	222	397	281	176	449	73	107	71	156	123	

R2 *Mileage chart*

Country	Visa required	Country	Visa required	Country	Visa required
Algiers	no	Greece[e]	no	Portugal[e]	no
Australia	yes	Hungary	yes	Qatar[c]	no
Austria	no	Iceland[e]	no	Romania	yes
Bahamas	no	India	yes	Saudi Arabia	yes
Bahrain	no	Indonesia[d, k]	no	Seychelles[k]	no
Bangladesh	yes	Iraq	yes	Singapore[k]	no
Barbados[f, k]	no	Israel	no	South Africa[k]	yes
Belgium	no	Italy[e, k]	no	Spain	no
Bermuda[k]	no	Jamaica[f, k]	no	Sudan	yes
Botswana	no	Japan[f, k]	no	Sweden[e]	no
Brazil[a, k]	no	Jordan	yes	Switzerland	no
Bulgaria	yes	Kenya[j]	no	Syria	yes
Canada[j]	no	Kuwait	yes	Tanzania[g]	no
Cape Verde	yes	Lebanon	yes	Thailand	yes
China	yes	Liberia	yes	Tunisia	no
Columbia[e, k]	no	Luxembourg[k]	no	Turkey	no
Cote D'Ivoire	no	Malawi	no	Uganda	yes
Cyprus[e]	no	Malaysia[e, k]	no	United Arab	
Czechoslovakia	yes	Malta[e]	no	Emirates[c]	no
Denmark[e]	no	Mauritius[e, k]	no	USA[c, k]	no
Egypt	yes	Morocco[e]	no	USSR	yes
Ethiopia	yes	Netherlands[e]	no	Venezuela[h, k]	no
Finland[e]	no	New Zealand[e, k]	no	Yemen Arab Rep	yes
France[j]	no	Nigeria	yes	Yugoslavia[k]	no
Gambia[k]	no	Oman	yes	Zaire	yes
Germany	no	Pakistan	yes	Zambia[i]	no
Ghana	yes	Philippines[b, k]	no	Zimbabwe[k]	no
Gibraltar	no	Poland	yes		

[a] Business visa required
[b] Visa not required for stay up to 21 days
[c] Visa not required for stay up to 30 days
[d] Visa not required for stay up to 2 months
[e] Visa not required for stay up to 3 months
[f] Visa not required for stay up to 6 months
[g] Visitor's pass needed
[h] Tourist card needed
[i] Visitors not holding return tickets or required documents for onward travel will need to pay a deposit to the Immigration Authorities.
[j] Visitors may be required to show evidence of onward or return tickets.
[k] Return or onward ticket needed.

R3 *Information on visa requirements*

Country	Currency	Dialling from UK	Dialling code to UK	Time based on 1200 hrs GMT 1300 hrs BST
Australia	Dollars	010 61*	001144	2000 (Perth)
Austria	Schillings	01043*	0044	1300 hrs
Belgium	Francs	01032	00...44	1300 hrs
Canada	Dollars	010 1*	01144	0700 (Montreal)
Denmark	Kroner	010 45	00944	1300 hrs
France	Francs	010 33 010 331 (Paris)	19...44	1300 hrs
Germany	Marks	010 37 (East)* 010 49 (West)*	0044	1300 hrs
Greece	Drachmae	010 30*	0044	1400 (Athens)
Holland	Guilders	010 31*	09...44	1300 hrs
Hong Kong	Dollars	010 852*	00144	2000 hrs
India	Rupee	010 91*	0044	1730 hrs
Israel	Shekels	010 972*	0044	1400 (Jerusalem)
Italy	Lire	010 39*	0044	1300
Malta	Pounds	010 356	0044	1300
New Zealand	Dollars	010 64*	0044	2400
Norway	Kroner	010 47*	09544	1300 hrs
Portugal	Escudos	010 351*	0044	GMT
South Africa	Rand	010 27*	0944	1400 (Cape Town)
Spain	Pesetas	010 34*	07...44	1300 hrs
Sweden	Kronor	010 46*	00944	1300 hrs
Switzerland	Francs	010 41*	0044	1300 hrs
USA	Dollars	010 1*	01144	0700 (New York)
USSR	Ruble	010 7*	81044	1500 (Moscow)

Dialling from UK * = International code followed by area code, see International Dialling Code Book.
Dialling to UK ... = wait for second dialling tone. Follow the international dialling code with the national UK code, omitting the initial 0.

R4 *Travel guide to currency, time and dialling codes*

WEIGHT	**LENGTH**	**LIQUID VOLUME**
1 g = 0.04 oz 1 kg = 2.2 lb	1 mm = 0.04 in 1 cm = 0.39 in 1 m = 3.28 ft 1 km = 0.62 mile	1 ml = 0.04 fl oz 1 l = 1.76 pt 1 l = 0.22 gal
1 oz = 28.35 g 1 lb = 0.45 kg	1 in = 2.54 cm 1 ft = 0.30 m 1 yd = 0.91 m 1 mile = 1.61 km	1 fl oz = 28.41 ml 1 pt = 0.57 l 1 gal = 4.55 l

g = gram
kg = kilogram
oz = ounce
lb = pounds

mm = millimetre
cm = centimetre
m = metre
km = kilometre
in = inch
ft = foot
yd = yard

ml = millilitre
l = litre
fl oz = fluid ounce
pt = pint
gal = gallon

R5 *Imperial and metric conversion tables*

A3 Paper
297 mm long × 420 mm wide

Computer listing paper
Tables: financial
Notices
Advertisements

A4 Paper
297 mm long
× 210 mm wide

Letters
A4 Memoranda
Reports
Commonly used for
photocopying

A5 Paper
Landscape
148 mm long ×
210 mm wide

A5 Paper
Portrait
210 mm long
× 148 mm wide

Often used for memoranda,
short letters, small notices

Portrait has the shorter edge at the top

Landscape has the longer edge at the top

A6   148 mm long
      × 105 mm wide

Postcards
Reminder cards
Appointment cards
Index cards

A7   74 mm long
      × 105 mm wide

Business cards

R6 *International paper sizes*

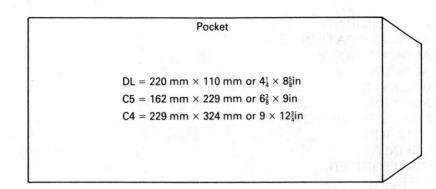

Pocket

DL = 220 mm × 110 mm or $4\frac{1}{4}$ × $8\frac{5}{8}$in
C5 = 162 mm × 229 mm or $6\frac{3}{8}$ × 9in
C4 = 229 mm × 324 mm or 9 × $12\frac{3}{4}$in

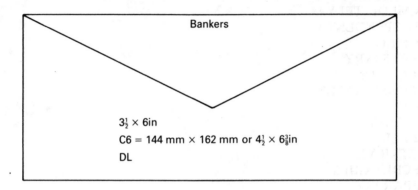

Bankers

$3\frac{1}{2}$ × 6in
C6 = 144 mm × 162 mm or $4\frac{1}{2}$ × $6\frac{3}{8}$in
DL

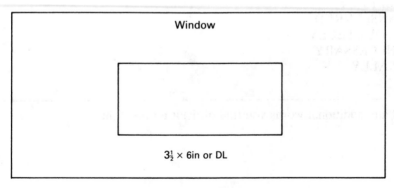

Window

$3\frac{1}{2}$ × 6in or DL

DL most commonly used business envelope, A4 folded × 3
C6 suitable for an A6 unfolded sheet
C5 suitable for an A5 unfolded sheet
C4 suitable for an A4 unfolded sheet

R7 *Envelope types and sizes*

ACCOMMODATE
ACCOMMODATION
ACQUAINTANCE
ACQUIRE
BELIEVED
BUSINESS
CORRESPONDENCE
DECISION
DEFINITE
DISAPPOINTED
ESPECIALLY
EXPENSES
EXTREMELY
IMMEDIATELY
INDEPENDENT
LOSING
NECESSARY
OCCASION
OCCASIONALLY
OCCURRED
RECEIVE
REFERRED
RETRIEVE
SECRETARIES
SEPARATE
SEPARATELY
SINCERELY
TRANSFERRED
UNDOUBTEDLY
UNNECESSARY
USUALLY

Add any additional words you find difficult on the right.

R8 *Common misspellings*

The apostrophe is frequently misused and misunderstood, but if used correctly in written communications, it greatly enhances the professional image of an organization.

1. The apostrophe is used to indicate **possession**. If a singular noun, ie one person, one thing, then 's is used.

   Dr Wilson's bag (the bag belongs to Dr Wilson)
   The company's directors (the directors belong to the company)
   The boss's diary
   The author's book
   The customer's account
   The student's handbook

   If it is a plural noun, ie more than one person or thing, then just an apostrophe is added at the end.

   Doctors' bags (the bags belong to the doctors)
   Companies' accounts (accounts belonging to more than one company)
   Customers' addresses
   Students' books

   But for plurals that do not end in 's' add 's, eg children's books.

2. The apostrophe is also used to indicate missing letter(s).

   one o'clock (one of the clock)
   isn't (is not)
   they're (they are)
   it's (it is)

   Apart from the first accepted example, it is unusual to use an apostrophe for this purpose in business correspondence as abbreviated expressions should not be used.

R9 *Use of the apostrophe*

Correction signs are used when proof-reading handwritten or typewritten work and alterations need to be made. Alterations are indicated both in the margin and in the text as in the example given:

Correction	Sign in margin	Sign in text
Capital letters (upper case)	uc /or CAPS	Two lines under the character/words to be <u>corrected</u>.
Small letters (lower case)	lc/	One line under the character/words to be <u>corrected</u>.
Insert a new paragraph	NP/	Square bracket in text at start of new paragraph. ⊏
Do not begin a new paragraph	run on/	⟩ between ⟨ paragraphs
Insert the word(s) which has been incorrectly crossed out.	stet /	.... under word(s) to be inserted.
Insert a space	⚏	∧ where the space is to go.
Insert a word/character	word or character	∧
Close up a space	⊐/	⊃ in text
Change the words or letters around	trs/	The ⌐Review⌐Annual⌐
Delete (take out) characters or words crossed out.	⌀⟩	Word crossed ~~out~~.

Note: The oblique line after the sign shows it is the end of the correction.

stet = let it stand.
trs = transpose.

R10 *Proof-reading correction signs*

INDEX

This book is due for return on or before the last date shown below.